MW01089292

ACTIVE COLLECTIONS

In recent years, many museums have implemented sweeping changes in how they engage audiences. However, changes to the field's approaches to collections stewardship have come much more slowly. *Active Collections* critically examines existing approaches to museum collections and explores practical, yet radical, ways that museums can better manage their collections to actively advance their missions.

Approaching the question of modern museum collection stewardship from a position of "tough love," the authors argue that the museum field risks being constrained by rigid ways of thinking about objects. Examining the field's relationship to objects, artifacts, and specimens, the volume explores the question of stewardship through the dissection of a broad range of issues, including questions of "quality over quantity," emotional attachment, dispassionate cataloging, and cognitive biases in curatorship. The essays look to insights from fields as diverse as forest management, library science, and the psychology of compulsive hoarding, to inform and innovate collection practices.

Essay contributions come from both experienced museum professionals and scholars from disciplines as diverse as psychology, education, and history. The result is a critical exploration that makes essential reading for museum professionals, as well as those in training.

Elizabeth Wood is Professor of museum studies, and public scholar of museums, families, and learning at Indiana University-Purdue University Indianapolis (IUPUI), USA.

Rainey Tisdale is an independent curator who leads for change on field-wide issues including place-based interpretation, collections stewardship, creative practice, and museums and well-being.

Trevor Jones is Director and CEO of the Nebraska State Historical Society, USA.

ACTIVE COLLECTIONS

Edited by Elizabeth Wood, Rainey Tisdale and Trevor Jones

Routledge
Taylor & Francis Group

NEW YORK AND LONDON

First published 2018
by Routledge
711 Third Avenue, New York, NY 10017

and by Routledge
2 Park Square, Milton Park, Abingdon, Oxon, OX14 4RN

Routledge is an imprint of the Taylor & Francis Group, an informa business

© 2018 Taylor & Francis

The right of Elizabeth Wood, Rainey Tisdale and Trevor Jones to be identified as the authors of the editorial material, and of the authors for their individual chapters, has been asserted in accordance with sections 77 and 78 of the Copyright, Designs and Patents Act 1988.

Library of Congress Cataloging-in-Publication Data
A catalog record for this book has been requested

ISBN: 978-1-62958-522-2 (hbk)
ISBN: 978-1-62958-523-9 (pbk)
ISBN: 978-1-315-14515-0 (ebk)

Typeset in Bembo
by Swales & Willis Ltd, Exeter, Devon, UK

DEDICATION

To museum collections everywhere, we love you but . . .

CONTENTS

ILLUSTRATIONS

Figures

Tables

Boxes

CONTRIBUTORS

Paul Bourcier is the Curator at the Museum of Science and History in Jacksonville, FL. He previously served as Chief Curator at the Wisconsin Historical Society and is co-editor of *Nomenclature 4.0 for Museum Cataloging*.

Kate Bowell is a museologist specializing in the intersection of people, stories, and objects. With degrees in zoology, literature, and museum science, her experience crosses multiple disciplines. Working with natural history, archaeological, and historical museums, Kate specializes in interpretive development, experience design, and visitor studies. Her previous work includes planning and development for the Fort Collins Museum of Discovery, public interpretation of the Lindenmeier Site National Historic Landmark, and the opening of History Colorado. As a museum consultant, author, and presenter, Kate has worked with organizations throughout North America and Europe. Kate can be found at www.museumsaskew.com and @museumsaskew.

Benjamin Filene is Director of Public History and Professor of History at the University of North Carolina at Greensboro. Prior to UNCG, Filene was Senior Exhibit Developer at the Minnesota Historical Society, where he served as lead developer on the award-winning exhibition *Open House: If These Walls Could Talk*. He co-edited the collection *Letting Go? Historical Authority in a User-Generated World* (2011). Since 2006, Filene has worked with his graduate students to complete a series of community-based, collaborative projects, and he has consulted on exhibition projects across the country.

Mark A. Greene is Senior Archivist Emeritus at University of Wyoming; for 13 years he directed the American Heritage Center there, one of the nation's largest university-based archival repositories. He previously headed research center programs at The Henry Ford museum; among other responsibilities supervising the museum registrar's department. Earlier he spent 11 years as curator of manuscripts at the Minnesota Historical Society, where he worked closely with the Society's museum curators. During his 30-year career he published 27 peer-reviewed articles in seven nations. He served as president of the Society of American Archivists and became a Distinguished Fellow in 2002.

Susan M. Irwin is Director of Library & Archives Division at the Arizona Historical Society. Ms. Irwin received her MBA from the University of Portland, an MA in Information Resources and Library Science from the University of Arizona, and is a doctoral candidate in History at Arizona State University. She served on the Collective Wisdom: Libraries, Archives, and Museums Conference Exchange national committee exploring the practices, cultures, and connections across the three professions and how they can inform each other. She has served as Chair of the Society of American Archivists' Committee on Education; Chair of the Arizona Library Association's Government Information Interest Group; and Secretary of the Maricopa County Library Council.

Robert R. Janes is an independent scholar-practitioner and served as Editor-in-Chief of the *Journal of Museum Management and Curatorship* from 2003 to 2014. He is also a visiting research fellow at the School of Museum Studies at the University of Leicester (United Kingdom). Janes has devoted his career to championing museums as important social institutions that are capable of making a difference in the lives of individuals and their communities. His latest book is *Museums without Borders* (2016)—a collection of nearly 40 years of his writing.

Trevor Jones is Director and CEO of the Nebraska State Historical Society. He believes that museum collections have the power to tell amazing stories, and has helped museums of all sizes rethink how artifact collections support their mission. Trevor holds BA degrees in History and German from Grinnell College, an MA degree in History and Certificate in Museum Studies from the University of Wisconsin-Milwaukee, and Project Management Professional (PMP) certification from the Project Management Institute.

Anne Jordan is a recent graduate from the IUPUI Museum Studies master's program, specializing in museum education. Her interests include live historical interpretation techniques, educational programming, and assessing accessibility needs at historic sites and institutions. She has worked all over the country including Colonial Williamsburg and the Benjamin Harrison Presidential Site. History is her passion and she hopes to continue to inspire others to understand the importance and relevance of learning about our past.

Modupe Labode is an associate professor of history and museum studies at Indiana University-Purdue University Indianapolis, where she is also a Public Scholar of African American History and Museums. Before coming to IUPUI in 2007, she was the chief historian at the Colorado Historical Society and taught at Iowa State University.

Masum Momaya is an independent scholar and research fellow at the Chicago Council on Global Affairs. She has curated exhibitions for the Smithsonian Asian

Pacific American Center and the International Museum of Women and published widely on the topics of race and immigration, women's rights, economic justice, and social justice. She earned an AB in Feminist Studies and Public Policy from Stanford University and both an EdM in Education and an EdD in Human Development from Harvard University.

Katherine Rieck is the Assistant Director of Education at Plains Art Museum in Fargo, North Dakota. Katherine holds an MA in Museum Studies from Indiana University-Purdue University Indianapolis and BAs in English and History from St. Olaf College in Northfield, Minnesota. Her work focuses on building creative and critical thinking from museum visits.

Gail Steketee is Dean and Professor Emerita at the Boston University School of Social Work. Her research has focused on developing and testing treatments for obsessive compulsive spectrum disorders, including OCD, body dysmorphic disorder, and hoarding disorder. She has published over 200 articles and chapters, and more than a dozen books on these topics. She is an elected Fellow of the American Academy of Social Work and Social Welfare and received the Outstanding Career Achievement Award from the International OCD Foundation in 2013.

Vickie Stone is the Registrar/Curator of Collections at the Coronado Historical Association. She is a graduate of the Museum Studies program at Indiana University-Purdue University Indianapolis. As a student she served as the Clowes Museum Fellow in the collections department at the Eiteljorg Museum of American Indians and Western Art. Her professional interests include making museum collections active, accessible, and inclusive through database/knowledge-base system management, alternative object care practice, and collaborative curation.

Gabriel Taylor is an emerging museum professional from Atlanta, GA. He has recently received a Master's of Arts degree in Museum Studies from Indiana University, School of Liberal Arts, Indianapolis. He has a BA in History from Spring Hill College in Mobile, AL. Gabe was raised in northern Alabama and is the youngest of five children. His professional focus is in creating unique and memorable experiences for museum audiences.

Rainey Tisdale is an independent curator who leads for change on field-wide issues including place-based interpretation, collections stewardship, creative practice, and museums and well-being. She has held curatorial positions at the AFL-CIO's museum, the US Senate's Office of Senate Curator, and the Bostonian Society; she was a Fulbright Scholar in Helsinki, Finland and a community fellow at Brown University's John Nicholas Brown Center for Public Humanities; and she taught in the Museum Studies Program at Tufts University. She is an international expert on city museums and a co-founder of the Active Collections project. With Linda Norris, she co-authored *Creativity in Museum Practice* (2013).

Linda A. Whitaker is a certified archivist and librarian for the Arizona Historical Society at Papago Park in Tempe. Ms. Whitaker has served in various local, regional, and national leadership positions. She was a member of the Editorial

Advisory Board for *Managing Congressional Collections* and was a contributor to *Doing Archival Research in Political Science*. She is past Chair of the Society of American Archivists Congressional Papers Roundtable. She was the lead archivist for processing the Personal and Political Papers of Senator Barry Goldwater, the Stephen Shadegg Collection, and the Dennis DeConcini Papers. Ms. Whitaker is a founding member of the Arizona Archives Summit, a federally funded initiative to promote statewide collaborative collecting, now in its tenth year.

Elizabeth Wood is director of the Museum Studies Program at Indiana University-Purdue University Indianapolis (IUPUI), professor of museum studies, and public scholar of museums, families, and learning with The Children's Museum of Indianapolis. Wood's research includes the study of visitor-object experiences in museums, object-based learning, critical museum pedagogy, and evaluation capacity building. She is co-author of *The Objects of Experience: Transforming Visitor-Object Encounters in Museums* with Kiersten F. Latham (2014) and joined the Active Collections project in 2014.

FOREWORD

Jim Vaughn

The one constant in our museum world is change.

In my more than four decades of museum experience, I have witnessed a continuous series of changes in the policies and practices that guide museums and historic sites. Audience studies, computer technology, digital photography, conservation advances, new exhibition philosophies, progressive educational ideals, cell phones, and social media—all of these developments, as well as a variety of external societal pressures and the shifting balance between connoisseurship and social history, have greatly altered the way we collect and what we collect. All too often, however, our professional standards and expectations related to the management and use of our collections have lagged behind in our rapidly changing world.

When I first entered the history and museum profession in the 1970s, I quickly accepted the concept that our base mission was fundamentally to collect, preserve, and interpret artifacts, manuscripts, and even buildings "in perpetuity." My generation spent a lot of energy and debate in those early years establishing collections policies and procedures, creating the complex legal and ethical framework for accessioning and deaccessioning, and setting "professional standards" for collection records, environments, and security. I think we naively assumed that these policies and procedures also would last "in perpetuity."

In the 1970s, I did not fully recognize that the museum profession was so young and that we were, in fact, writing standards and creating high expectations that were yet to be tested by the practical realities of museum operations. In our efforts to establish professional standards, we may have enshrined them as unchallengeable truths too soon. I think experience has taught many of us that "in perpetuity" is a very long time.

Even as we were making what we thought were to be long-standing rules, the museum world was changing. I clearly remember the day that we opened the boxes containing our first desktop computer—an Apple III—and we contemplated the creation of an electronic database to replace our decades of paper collection records. What other changes would follow?

Over four decades of museum and preservation experience, I found I was continually confronted by the impracticality—and sometimes the impossibility—of achieving accepted professional standards in managing collections. There was never enough time, money, or staff. It did not take long in practice for all of us to see that it was a lot easier to add to collections than to deaccession from them and that many museums were being overwhelmed by continually growing collections without the means to adequately care for them.

Experience is always the best teacher. My own experience led me to doubt the wisdom of a number of these foundational beliefs. Standards and rules often define matters in black and white, but managing collections, especially history collections, involves many shades of gray and requires a lot of situational decision-making and common sense. By mid-career, like so many museum professionals of my generation, I began to do a lot of rethinking.

In 2002 and 2007, I hosted two conferences about "Rethinking the Historic House Museum." The participants concluded, among other things, that returning some of these museum houses to private ownership was sometimes the more effective way to assure the continued preservation of these important community resources for future generations. Might this also be true for many museum artifacts, stored in less than ideal conditions, slowly deteriorating, and seldom, if ever, seen by the public?

In 2007, in an article for *Museum* magazine entitled "Rethinking the Rembrandt Rule," I challenged the idea that we should treat all objects with the same level of care and protection. To my surprise the article resonated with many other museum professionals.

As I reflect on my experience, I am convinced that we all need to spend more time challenging and rethinking all of the practices and policies that shape our daily work assumptions. I personally have been very encouraged over the past few years as I have seen more and more recognition by the profession that different situations require different approaches and solutions. An excellent example is the American Alliance of Museums' *Direct Care of Collections: Ethics, Guidelines and Recommendations* (April 2016), which addresses the long-debated question of the ethical use of deaccession proceeds.

As more and more museums make their collections available on the Internet, we will necessarily continue to rethink the way we do business. I have already seen the impact of digital access here at the Pennsylvania State Archives. Five years ago, we served about 4,000 users per year. Since then, we have digitized and put online more that 14 million manuscripts and last year we served more than 4.5 million distinct users on the Internet.

Online museum collections will also expand our reach and provide many new opportunities for museums. I can envision collecting consortiums in which multiple institutions develop collaborative and coordinated collecting strategies to reduce duplication, lower costs, and simultaneously increase access to artifacts. Greater access could reduce the perceived value of ownership. It might also diminish the argument for building study collections if artifacts from many different institutions can be easily analyzed and compared online.

I can also imagine sunset acquisitions, in which many, if not most, artifacts are accessioned for a specific number of years and then automatically deaccessioned, unless a proactive decision is made to renew the accession. This would force us to continually reevaluate our collections.

One of our biggest challenges continues to be refining and reducing the collections that we already have. Because of the labor and legal issues involved, it is almost always easier and cheaper to keep items than to deaccession them. But now, at least, it is widely accepted that responsible historical organizations will periodically assess and thin their collections.

In the chapters that follow, you will see that many individuals and institutions are actively rethinking collection issues and moving in directions that we would not have considered just a decade or two ago. I am delighted to see a younger generation of museum professionals challenging many of the standard assumptions about collections that may have served us well at one time, but now need to be rethought. In the rapidly changing word of museums, we need flexible and practical approaches to managing collections.

I think you may be encouraged, even surprised, by some of the new directions reflected in these articles. I see them as reassuring examples of a vibrant and constantly evolving profession.

References

American Alliance of Museums. 2016. *Direct Care of Collections: Ethics, Guidelines and Recommendations.* Available at http://aam-us.org/docs/default-source/default-document-library/direct-care-of-collections-ethics-guidelines-and-recommendations-pdf.pdf?sfvrsn=8.

Vaughn, James M. 2008. "Rethinking the Rembrandt Rule." *Museum* 87 (2): 33–35, 71.

INTRODUCTION

Trevor Jones, Rainey Tisdale, and Elizabeth Wood

This book is a compilation of essays, ideas, and inspirations that stem from the Active Collections project, a grassroots effort to generate discussion and action across the museum field to develop a new approach to collections, one that is more effective and sustainable. Our goal in presenting this volume is an attempt to reconcile museum visitors' contemporary relationships to the material world with museum practices that desperately need to be updated.

Modifications to best practices for collections have lagged behind other areas of museum practice. As a field, we are working to make museums more inclusive, more audience-centered, and better equipped to engage in dialogue. This shift, often driven by museum educators but increasingly embraced by all types of museum workers, stems from a recognition that our audiences have changed and that we need to change with them in order to remain relevant. Where museum collections are concerned, however, change has come much more slowly. With their collections, museums have traditionally stressed that they will be preserved forever, and perhaps because of this commitment we have preserved how we think about collections as well. For museum collections, relevance is about ensuring that the collection serves the mission, relates to the museum's audiences, and has a viable life beyond the storeroom walls in exhibitions and programs. By neglecting to see the changing role of collections as part of an ongoing discussion in museum practice, it's as if we are upgrading the furniture and putting new paint on the walls while neglecting to go into the basement to repair a crumbling foundation.

Trevor once visited a vibrant city museum in the southwest of America where over 90% of the audience was Latinx. The museum had engaging educational programs, bilingual exhibitions exploring contemporary lives, and a website focused on the culture of the city's immigrant groups. Its collections were a different story. The storerooms were crammed with items from the wealthy White elite who had founded the museum, and these collections now had little relevance to the current audience. The museum was spending so much time and effort trying to deal with these legacy collections that staff had minimal capacity or space to collect those things that were relevant to the city's present and future. When Trevor suggested that they deaccession almost all of these legacy collections in order to make room for new ones more relevant to the city's majority population, the response was, "We can't do that, we promised to care for them forever." If collections are to be truly valuable in shaping and driving the stories, ideas, and values we present to the public, then our collections practices need to change along with the rest of the museum.

Anyone who has spent some time in museum practice will know that changing our approach to collections is no simple task. There are a multitude of factors that come into play—legal, ethical, institutional, logistical, financial, human. If this process were easy, we would have dealt with it a long time ago. But just because it's hard doesn't let us off the hook. And by us we mean all of us, because the collection should be every museum worker's responsibility. Imagine, for example, if educators—our visitor advocates, and the ones who often end up interpreting collections objects for the public—had a voice in acquisition and deaccession decisions. This is just one of the complicated changes in practice we are discussing as part of the Active Collections project.

Who Are We to Write This Book?

We've been working in the museum field for years (see our bios for the details), but no one deputized us to try and rethink how museums think about objects. We were frustrated about museums' relationship to the things in their collections and decided we wanted to stop complaining about it and instead push for meaningful change. We are questioning and agitating from a position of tough love. As longtime collections people, we passionately believe in the power of objects, and our goal here is to enhance their meaning, vitality, and use—not throw them out with the proverbial bathwater. We are not alone in this stance: by talking to a wide range of colleagues and reading broadly—both the US museum literature and the literature from other countries—we have realized there are plenty of other museum workers who are looking for new ways to work with collections as well. If you are reading this, chances are you are at least open to rethinking how museums, and by extension our society, deals with "stuff." We expect that you love objects too, and we hope that at least some of the essays in this book inspire you to channel that love toward a new vision of what collections need from us in order to live up to their full potential.

The Active Collections Story

When Rainey and Trevor started working on Active Collections in 2012, they initially followed a classic model for building support for their ideas. They sought out leaders in the field who might lend their weight and resources, describing their vision and trying to find an institutional home for a large-scale initiative that might flow from the top down. They attracted some modest interest, but they weren't building much momentum toward action. Then Rainey's work organizing Boston-area cultural organizations after the 2013 Marathon Bombing taught her that when you're trying to put forward a new approach people are uncertain about, you need to show, not tell. So they stopped trying to get anyone's blessing and instead started publishing and testing their ideas, giving them room to breathe and circulate among rank-and-file museum workers—a small-scale, bottom-up initiative. From the beginning, they were committed to radical ideas and big change. Thus, their first step was the Active Collections Manifesto (this volume). In 2014 Rainey and Trevor sent out drafts of the manifesto to a wide range of museum professionals. Elee was one of those recipients. Her first response: "I LOVE THIS!!!!! I'm ready to be your agent of dissemination." In fact, many of the reviewers had encouraging words for the project. There was a clear sense of need to dig deeper in several key areas of collections work. Deaccessioning was a particular sticking point: with so many complicated standards, ethical considerations, and action steps to take into account, there was a feeling that deaccessioning was creating a bottleneck in the overall approach to museum collections. Others felt the process of placing a "value" on collections needed to be addressed more carefully. It was clear that everyone has strong feelings about collections challenges overall, and the field could benefit from a forum to address collections issues in a new way. So Rainey and Trevor started that forum in the form of www.activecollections.org. There you can participate by contributing thought pieces, case studies, and tools. Shortly after the website launched in the fall of 2014, Elee joined the collaboration and together we began working to build the case for Active Collections and to put our ideas into practice.

Our original focus was history museums, because they are numerous and tend to have large collections, very small budgets, and difficulty adhering to focused collecting scopes. As the project grew we began hearing from art curators, archivists, and archaeologists who had similar concerns about storing and using collections. Some of our discussions and research began to embrace parallels with compulsive hoarding, practices in forestry management, and much more. Our focus on history museums remains evident, but this book should be of use to multiple disciplines.

Since 2014, we have conducted a nationwide deaccessioning survey for museums of all types, facilitated discussions about Active Collections at museum conferences and gatherings across the country, and written multiple grants to test out ideas.

One of the most fulfilling aspects of this project has been our collaborative, interdisciplinary approach. We each come from a different orientation to museum work—Rainey as a curator, Trevor as an administrator and collections manager, Elee as an educator and evaluator. We share the philosophy that museums are fundamentally about people and about use, but we approach that philosophy from different angles. In other words, Active Collections is a big tent. Our most fervent hope is that others will test out ideas, come up with their own solutions, and join us in changing museum practice bit by bit.

Why Now Is the Time for Some Tough Love

In 2015, we hosted a Future of Museum Collections Roundtable with several museum scholars and practitioners. Noted museum scholar and critic Jay Rounds suggested during one of the sessions that a book like this comes about because of a paradigm shift. All paradigms are just sets of standards, perspectives, and ideas that focus on a core issue or problem. Over time more and more ideas get layered onto this way of thinking. Then, at the height of each paradigm, the big idea at its core solidifies into a dominant model that everyone follows, and the system becomes very efficient but also very rigid. Eventually the world changes enough that the dominant model stops working and slowly starts to be dismantled, producing a crisis. The period of the paradigm crisis is uncertain but also highly creative and energizing. Because museums are currently experiencing one of these paradigm shifts, we are just one of many projects organizing for change in the field. Everyone seems impatient and ready for change, but charting that path to change is difficult.

Paradigms about museum collections influence our practices and approaches to every aspect of museum work—whether it is through how and what museums collect; how collections are cared for and put on display; or how society values collections. Historically museums have been through several paradigms, and notably in each iteration our knowledge about collections has changed and evolved. Jay Rounds described three key paradigms affecting museum practice. First, in the nineteenth century, a museum collection was intended to reflect the work of God in creating the world—museums aimed to collect one of everything and to help the individual impose mental discipline to override their instinct, human nature, and affect. Then, in the twentieth century, museum collections were intended to be a tangible symbol of the dominant culture, and concepts like the theory of evolution influenced the idea of collecting not only one of everything but one of everything at every stage to show evolutionary changes and progress. Finally, today, our society is entering a new paradigm. The theories of social determinism are falling apart as people acquire, use, and discard different cultures instead of being socialized into them. We acknowledge people do not internalize culture as much as we previously thought and an individual's varied cultural background is valued over "melting pot" assimilation. Despite these changes in perspective, no persuasive explanation for how social order can arise out of difference rather than sameness exists yet. Until it does we will stay in paradigm crisis.

We recognize that the essays in this book present competing and sometimes even contradictory notions on how to deal with the problems we face with collections—that's what happens in the middle of a paradigm crisis. We are trying to influence policy and practice in a situation where there are conflicting values, and thus we need to be careful not to choose one or the other but instead look for ways to reconcile them. Throughout the book we have asked contributors to reflect on and pose questions about the values of the museum field that are coming into conflict, the ones the paradigm shift needs to reconcile. This is not a book with all the answers; it's a book that seeks to help us find them.

How to Use this Book

Active Collections can either be read in order, or by theme. The book is divided into two sections: *Conceptual Frameworks* and *New Ideas and Tools for Change*. Because many of these essays stem from discussions during the Future of Museum Collections Roundtable we convened in 2015, readers will notice some commonalities about the nature of collections, and especially our need to rethink how we acquire, manage, and interpret them. However, each author has approached the problem from a different angle, stemming from their own viewpoint and expertise.

The chapters in *Section I: Conceptual Frameworks* focus on big ideas surrounding collections and their role in society. You will find different and sometimes provocative frameworks, approaches, and ideas about collections—both in the museum field and in other fields. Our goal for this section is to constructively question the theories, values, and assumptions we make about our collections, and suggest ways we might change our thinking to better serve the public good.

Masum Momaya provides a list of strategies to consider how we can actively work to make our collections anti-racist and anti-colonialist. Rainey Tisdale investigates current trends and phenomena, and what it means to truly serve the needs of today's museum audiences as they grapple with enormous change in the world around us. Modupe Labode observes and analyzes the relationship between things and feelings in the public sphere. Gail Steketee looks at the psychology of compulsive hoarding and how it compares to museum collections and their relationships with "stuff." Elizabeth Wood explores the potential of collections as living systems and how other disciplines manage "collections" in the natural world. Mark A. Greene reflects on the impact of his transformational "More Product Less Process" model for the archival world and what it means today. Robert Janes finishes the section by questioning our complicated relationship with things, and museum sustainability in a changing world.

In *Section II: New Ideas and Tools for Change* we look at new practices, exploring how museums might work with collections if they weren't so bound to long-held assumptions. If you are looking for practical applications to help make your collections more active, start here. Trevor Jones focuses on ways to tier (or rank) your collections based on how well they support the mission. Paul Bourcier tackles the assumptions of collections catalogs and looks at how our efforts to classify and catalog collections are bound by our assumptions, and offers some ways to rethink the current model. Based on her knowledge of compulsive hoarding, Gail Steketee provides a fresh perspective as to why letting go of objects is so hard for museum workers and uses the tools of a psychologist to offer help. Benjamin Filene explores constructivist models of collecting and evaluates where we go from here. Susan Irwin and Linda Whitaker use two case studies from their archival work in Arizona to show how new ways of thinking can transform institutions while increasing access to collections. Finally, Kate Bowell imagines a world where unloved objects have new life as something magical. Her creative take on the use of museum collections within the community offers an exciting pathway for object use.

Interspersed throughout the book are a series of "interludes" that are intended as short think pieces. They are meant to be provocations on current practice, inspirations from other fields, or new takes on classic ideas. They are intentionally spunky, spirited, and a bit irreverent.

Continuing the Conversation

The conversation to make collections more active should be a field-wide effort, but we know that the best change starts by talking with others about your ideas. Consider how this book, or particular chapters, can find their way into staff meetings or a full-scale book discussion. If you are a manager or director, consider how the issues raised here can provide guiding questions to get staff seriously thinking about new strategies.

If you are intrigued, incensed, or inspired by anything you read here, let us know about it. We can be reached via www.activecollections.org. Although we've chosen the more traditional format of a book, we see these essays as part of an ongoing dialogue rather than the end of the conversation. As time goes by we hope that others will find ways to improve on these ideas and make them their own. We believe the way to make things better is to experiment, question, and always seek better ways to do things. We believe passionately in the power of museum artifacts to inspire and change lives, and we hope you will contribute to making a greater impact for the field.

Acknowledgments

This project was made possible, in part, through funding provided by Indiana University's New Frontiers in the Arts and Humanities-New Currents grant program. Additional support was provided by the Museum Studies Program at Indiana University-Purdue University Indianapolis in the School of Liberal Arts, and the IUPUI Center for Service and Learning.

We wish to thank all our contributors, peer reviewers, friends, and family for helping make this book possible. In particular we are grateful for the contributions of Erik Peterson in support of the book production. We are also appreciative of the hundreds of colleagues across the museum field who have strengthened this effort with your stories and experience from the trenches, your questions and arguments, your ideas and experiments, and your own advocacy on behalf of Active Collections. Your commitment to making museums better inspires us every day.

A MANIFESTO FOR ACTIVE HISTORY MUSEUM COLLECTIONS

Trevor Jones and Rainey Tisdale

This manifesto first appeared on the Active Collections website in 2014.

Millions of artifacts in museum collections across the country are not actively supporting the institutions that steward them. Museums of all types are experiencing this problem, but it is particularly entrenched in history museums. Most history museums possess thousands of poorly maintained, inadequately cataloged, and underutilized artifacts. Instead of being active assets, these lazy artifacts drain vital resources. Multiple studies have assessed the problem of collections preservation, and each has proposed providing museums more money to process and preserve artifacts. But there's little point in preserving collections if they don't actively support the mission. **We believe collections must either advance the mission or they must go.**

Collections are expensive. The time and money required to catalog and store objects ties up valuable resources that could be used elsewhere. Fortunately, museum professionals are recognizing that significant portions of their collections aren't pulling their weight, and attitudes are changing. But in the absence of a coherent philosophy or way forward, changing opinions have not yet led to changes in practice. Therefore, the problem continues to get worse with each passing year. In addition, professional standards, funding models, and museum training programs still primarily support the idea that all collections are equally important, and that owning collections is as important as effectively using them. **We believe a new model for thinking about collections is needed.**

Collections are important to history museums. Artifacts are a deeply powerful way to connect with what it means to be human and to understand the past, present, and future. In his compelling book *A History of the World in 100 Objects* Neil MacGregor, Director of the British Museum, argues that "telling history through things is what museums are for" (2011, xiii). Museums are uniquely positioned to use things to tell meaningful stories—but to do so they need to collect the right artifacts and make good use of them. **We believe that artifacts can be powerful tools—touchstones filled with meaning and connection—but only when used effectively.**

If museums existed simply to preserve things, the best way to save them would be to put the entire collection in an enormous freezer and never take anything out. But museums don't just preserve things; they also *use* them to inspire, enlighten, and connect. Every day museums balance the twin needs of preservation and access. Every time a piece is used by a researcher or is exhibited, the decision has been made to shorten its lifespan. We weigh these decisions against the rarity of the piece, its condition, and how important it is to the institution. How is it that we distinguish degrees of significance when we deal with individual objects and yet we are paralyzed into inaction when we look at an entire collection? Major conservation surveys and statewide risk assessments assume that all collections are equally valuable and are worthy of the same standard of care. **We believe some objects support the mission better than others—not based on monetary value or rarity, but based on the stories they tell and the ideas they illuminate. The ones that provide the most public value should get the largest share of our time and resources.**

As museums have professionalized, we've touted care standards to donors and created the expectation all artifacts will be treated equally and be kept forever. Advancing the idea that all collections are equal and will always be cared for has become both a crutch to support an antiquated idea (museums exist to preserve things) and a stick to beat those who want to use artifacts in innovative ways (doing that would violate best practices!). The needs of the communities we serve shift over time, so why should museums care equally for artifacts that no longer meet the needs of our current audience? In our concern to preserve everything because we don't know what people in the future will find useful, we are diverting attention and care from objects that are useful right now to the people right in front of us. Museum professionals must change the conversation with boards, donors, and stakeholders about why and how artifacts help the institution meet its goals. Words matter, and we need new ones to talk about collections. **We believe we need to change the conversation from caring for artifacts to caring about people.**

We cannot continue to function in this manner. We live an era of hyper-consumption and production. Material goods are produced at a rate that was unimaginable when American museums first started collecting. We've got to change how and what we collect or we'll drown in consumer goods. Many history museums have chosen (whether consciously or not) to ignore the problem of collecting contemporary artifacts because of the high volume, but simply avoiding the problem is not a solution. If museums are to be more than hoarders, we need to deal with this issue. Museums are fond of telling donors about the size of the collection, equating size with quality. We leave them with the idea that simply getting more stuff makes us more relevant. **We need to stop touting the size of museum collections and start talking about impact.**

A Path toward Change

What if museums had smaller, more impactful collections, in which each object truly pulled its weight? Help the field move forward! Join us in finding out.

1. **Make Collections Everyone's Issue.** Discuss collections at the board level. Take your board into collections storage. Calculate what it costs to collect, preserve, and maintain your collections. Know the financial and personnel costs. Assess if your collections are active or lazy in supporting your mission.

2. **Initiate Smarter Sharing.** How many times has your institution acquired an object, not because it's unique or has an amazing story, but because it's a generic example that you might need someday for an exhibition? Wouldn't it be great if museums addressed this tendency (which fills countless storage rooms with lazy objects) by functioning like interlibrary loans? What if the museums in your region agreed to collect different artifacts, so that only one institution needed to have a few spinning wheels, for example, and everyone else was released from collecting them? If such a system existed, museums could focus on artifacts that tell important stories or their communities and borrow pieces easily from other institutions if they needed to. Start that conversation with museums in your area.

3. **Create a Tiered System for Your Collections.** Go ahead and rank your collections! What pieces best support the mission? What are the ones that are just ok? What really has NOTHING to do with what you're trying to accomplish? Establish a triage system for your artifacts and spend your time, effort, and money on the compelling ones.

4. **Change the Conversation.** Stop advertising the number of artifacts you have and start talking about their impact. Stop touting your role in preserving artifacts and instead talk about how you use them. Stop promising donors that you'll treasure their items forever. Start talking about a "useful life" for artifacts. Push funders and museum associations to stop tying funding and accolades to the number of artifacts preserved or cataloged. Instead ask to be assessed on how your collections are being used.

5. **Get Rid of What You Don't Need.** We need to make it easier for museums to deaccession their collections while preserving the public's trust. This is a complex and controversial issue, but it must be addressed or we will continue to misplace our priorities and hamstring efforts to provide public value. Current policies are too cumbersome and slow. Museums with collections that do not support their mission cannot be expected to jump through so many hoops that deaccessioning becomes a non-starter. We need streamlined, basic guidelines for mass deaccessions.

6. **Stop the Bleeding.** Do not accept artifacts you do not need. Start today. Get boards to understand that taking things you don't need drains resources from other areas. Make sure your collections committee and collecting plan are as

careful with new acquisitions as they are with deaccessions. Reject more than you take. "We might need it some day" is not a valid acquisition justification; it just leads you to death by a thousand cuts.

7. **Make the Good Stuff Sing.** Chances are you have artifacts that could tell incredible stories. Let them. Don't shoehorn them into an existing narrative and rob them of their power or bury them among hundreds of others. Pick a story and tell it. Be bold. All artifacts can be interpreted in many ways. Acknowledge this and choose one, the most compelling one. Don't water it down.

8. **Share Ideas.** Be part of a new breed of museum advocates who demand more from museum collections. Share these ideas and add your own. Put them into practice and tell others what works and what doesn't. Visit www. activecollections.org to share your experiences, tools, case studies, and additional resources.

Reference

MacGregor, Neil, 2011. *A History of the World in 100 Objects*. London: Viking.

SECTION I

Conceptual Frameworks

FIGURE 0.1A   Image by Ray Rieck (www.rayrieck.com)

1

TEN PRINCIPLES FOR AN ANTI-RACIST, ANTI-ORIENTALIST, ACTIVIST APPROACH TO COLLECTIONS

Masum Momaya

"Don't linger. Move along. There are lots of people behind us waiting to see this thing," my sister-in-law pleaded as she prodded my 12-year-old niece past the highly secured display case housing the Hope Diamond. My family had braved a long set of flights from India to Washington, DC to visit me at the Smithsonian while I was working there as a curator. A few days later, on a sticky summer Saturday, we faced the massive quasi-queue in the Gems Hall of the National Museum of Natural History (NMNH), taking our turn to "oooh" and "aaah" at one of the Institution's most visited and revered objects. Amongst the visitors to the jewel were many Indians and Indian Americans, who viewed the object with a sense of pride at its magnificence and stature within the Smithsonian's vast holdings.

With origins dating back to the 1600s in the Kollur mine in Golconda, India, the Hope Diamond was donated to the Smithsonian by Harry Winston Incorporated in 1958 (Smithsonian Encyclopedia 2003). Lore has it that French merchant Jean Baptiste Tavernier obtained an uncut, larger version of the stone and sold it to King Louis XIV of France. It made its way through the hands of other royalty, jewelers, thieves and collectors before finding its way to the Smithsonian (Smithsonian Encyclopedia 2003). The object's label describes a tiny bit of this provenance, but the context of how European empires generally acquired jewels from "the Orient" is entirely missing, on the object label and in the gallery as a whole.

Discussion of the diamond focuses primarily on its rare properties, its value as a scientific specimen, a supposed curse that it brings to those who own or wear it or the James Bond-esque tale of international intrigue that follows how it changed hands over centuries. Yet these conversations and the gem's positioning as a treasure in Smithsonian collections obscure the dubious and dishonest way in which many of today's museum treasures were acquired.[1] It is still unknown as to whether the Hope Diamond itself was bought or stolen. As with many objects acquired under the guise of exploration, transactional records, especially at the first point of exchange, are sparse, with documents simply delineating that the diamond was "obtained." Moreover, when this type of provenance information is murky, it's simply just left out of information that the museum shares with the public, rendering the theft of many objects invisible.

As a Smithsonian curator responsible for *Beyond Bollywood: Indian Americans Shape the Nation* (2014–2015), an exhibition about the history of Indian immigration in the United States, I often received questions about the Hope Diamond, including, "Is your exhibit in the gallery where the Hope Diamond is at?" and, "Why isn't the Hope Diamond in your exhibit?" *Beyond Bollywood* and the Hope Diamond were displayed in the same building in different galleries but were worlds apart conceptually. Still, visitors conflated the precious jewel from India with the history of Indian immigration and Indian Americans as if everything Indian was one massive entity, in the same way that some Americans and American media often refer to Africa as a monolithic entity devoid of a myriad of countries, cultures and peoples.

Amidst the widespread conflation, my niece posed a question that few, if any, other visitors were asking. Upon seeing the Hope Diamond, she asked loudly, "If it's from India like the label says, then why is it here? Shouldn't they give it back? It doesn't belong here. Is it *stolen*, mama?" "Shhhh!" my sister-in-law interceded. "Don't make a scene." Delightfully innocent and irreverent, my niece's brazen clarity stood in contrast to silence about provenance and contemporary methods of display and labeling that pervades many items within museum collections from "exotic" lands.

Unaware of the colonial legacies of museums as institutions, my niece's question came from curiosity about rightful ownership. Do museums have the right to collect whatever stuff they want wherever they encounter it? If so, under what circumstances? Should this "stuff" be labeled to reflect its provenance, murky, sordid or glamorous as it is? Or should it be given back to its place of origin, as my niece, as well as so many communities have asserted? Or, alternately, what if members of the community of origin want the object to remain in the museum because of the legitimacy and significance that museums confer on objects? And what if the community members know that a museum will care for an object better than any individual or other institution could? Given all of these questions, do we need a new way of collecting—and giving back—things in the twenty-first century? And if so, how could all the related practices of text and label writing, exhibit design, marketing, fundraising and public programming support a more conscientious collections strategy?

In the year and a half that *Beyond Bollywood* showed at NMNH, I walked hundreds of family members, friends and tourists through the galleries. Most of them accepted the Smithsonian's interpretations at face value. Amongst those of Indian origin, many were moved by the significance of their story being told in the world's largest, and arguably most well known, museum complex. Yet my niece's question about repatriation led me to wonder whether visitors take for granted institutional ownership and entitlement of objects with histories steeped in colonialism and racism.

These assumptions resonate all the way back to the first museums, which emerged in the sixteenth and seventeenth centuries as "cabinets of curiosities" for visitor amusement. Some of these curiosities, such as rhinoceros horns, elk antlers, shark teeth and human skin from unburied corpses, were thought to have medicinal healing powers (Alexander and Alexander 2008, 54). Later, these institutions became cabinets of natural history for systematic scientific study and display—to exhaustively catalog and understand the natural world and eventually the human place within it (Merriman 2008, 12).

This exhaustive cataloging was not only a scientific project, but also a cultural and political one. Burgeoning collections in museums demonstrated and cemented the European belief that knowledge can be embedded in organized material, and that material display creates knowledge and proper social relationships (Pearce 1995, 139). Displays evolved from shelves and cases of objects laid out in a rational order to dioramas which clustered and contextualized items, rendering impressions of "other" peoples of the world as both exotic and primitive.

As part of imperialism and colonialism, explorers and big game hunters traveled far and wide to amass tools, body ornaments, garments, housewares, animal skins and gems, eventually donating or selling them to museums. Many of Europe's largest museums acquired their collections in this way. For example, Captain James Cook and other explorers contributed specimens to the now vast anthropological and ethnographic collections of the British Museum (Alexander and Alexander 2008, 59). Large collections drawn from faraway lands conferred stature on institutions and empires. In this way, collecting from far and wide was a "fundamental element of the grand narrative explaining European supremacy" (Merriman 2008, 12).

In cementing these narratives through material displays, museums didn't just legitimize colonization; through the very act of collecting itself, they became *agents* of colonization. Museums' efforts helped define political boundaries as well as influence the social imagination of the museum-going public. This wasn't just true of European museums; museums in the Americas and Australia were guilty of these same practices with Native/indigenous peoples and people of color. Historically, museums worldwide have treated collections relating to people with disabilities in similar ways, substantiating notions of the "abnormal" through gawkish material displays (Sandell et al. 2005, 16). For example, objects such as a straightjacket used to restrain a person with a psychosocial disability, displayed without contextual information about the medicalization of disability or the pathological, racialized and gendered institutionalization of people with disabilities, reinforces the stereotype of "crazy" and leaves systemic oppression and pathologization unquestioned.

In the twenty-first century, museum collection practices have been called into question by communities that have long found themselves and their cultures pillaged, exoticized, stereotyped and maligned by museums. As Alexander and

Alexander point out, "travel, communication, and growing empowerment of the world's peoples have meant that the authority once proclaimed in natural history and anthropological museums has become at best dated and to some offensive" (2008, 74). What implications does the racist and orientalist history of museums and collections have for re-envisioning collections practices in the twenty-first century? How can we as museum professionals do our work in more conscientious ways? Acknowledging this history, I would like to propose ten principles for an anti-racist, anti-orientalist, activist approach to collections.

BOX 1.1 Ten Principles for an Anti-Racist, Anti-Orientalist, Activist Approach to Collections

1. Openly acknowledge legacies of colonialism, racism, oppression, distortion and theft.
2. Establish opportunities for community engagement, co-construction of meaning and destabilizing the notion of authority as residing in one party.
3. Aim for achieving "dissensus," or as many divergent perspectives as possible around a given object or collection rather than a consensus of singular narrative.
4. Accept that some communities view display of their histories in museums (problematic as they may be) as markers of arrival and legitimization.
5. Put repatriation and de-accessioning "on the table" as a part of collections policy, and loaning objects to community-based museums and local historical societies.
6. Prioritize collecting, and helping to preserve, objects endangered in humanitarian crises, natural disasters, violent conflict and war.
7. Reject definitions of value based on the grand narrative of European supremacy.
8. Consider how digital tools and social media shift the balance of power and voice and make these collections accessible.
9. Continuously question whether something must be collected and whether collected objects need to be saved versus repatriated, de-accessioned or disposed.
10. Situate collecting in the larger context of activist views/approaches to all of museum practice, including curating, visitor engagement, education, marketing and communications, fundraising, and management.

First, this new approach should openly acknowledge legacies of colonialism, racism, oppression, distortion and theft that are part of the founding of museums worldwide. Current museum professionals are not at fault for the perspectives and actions of their predecessors, but they can definitely be more conscientious about their practices going forward. For example, advertising grand and rare collections and marketing them as "Treasures of Imperial XX" or "Treasures of Ancient YY" without specifying the histories through which such objects were procured glorifies and legitimizes violent colonial history.

If we are going to keep such artifacts in our collections and display them in exhibitions, we should: (1) Be transparent, forthcoming and respectful around how they were acquired, including in our panel text, object labeling and marketing; (2) Initiate conversations with museums and communities in their place of origin and/or their diasporic communities in the United States, Canada, Australia and Europe about sharing artifacts and possibly repatriating them (see Conaty 2015); (3) Use revenues generated from such exhibitions to help build spaces, institutions and professional capacity to show, share and possibly repatriate these objects and works in their place of origin. The point is not to do away with these collections and exhibitions entirely but to engage with them critically as opportunities for more reflective and conscientious museum practice.

Second, an activist approach to collections should go hand in hand with community engagement, co-construction of meaning and destabilization of the notion of authority as residing in one party and needing to be deposited on everyone else. This parallels social science theories about knowledge being co-constructed as well as the tenets of coalition building in political organizing.[2] Today, curators and collections managers trained in social movement, critical and postcolonial theory are mindful of identity politics and the politics of representation. They strive to give voice to subjects and enable participatory decision making in interpretations. As Lynch and Alberti argue, "[s]hared authority is more effective at creating and guiding culture than institutional control" (2010, 15).

For instance, museums can issue open and public calls for submissions and convene collective conversations about what should be collected and why. Once objects are acquired museums can craft and save documentation and object records with multiple voices, beyond that of the lender and collector, when collecting and cataloging new collections. The Queens Museum in New York and Oakland Museum in California are known for their exemplary practice in this area, with the former employing community organizers as staff.

Third, an activist view of collections should aim for achieving "dissensus," or as many divergent perspectives as possible around a given object or collection rather than a consensus of singular narrative. The goal would be to build a community of interpretation with an intentional diversity of dissenting voices. For example, when collecting around #blacklivesmatter, could we aim for contrasting and perhaps even conflicting perspectives on this history? As Merriman (2008) suggests, collections can be thought of as opportunities for creation of relationships and ongoing dialogue rather than as possessions. The Smithsonian's Center for Folklife and Cultural Heritage used a mobile application to crowdsource descriptions of items suggested for collection and acquisition in its *The Will to Adorn* project on African American traditions of dress and body adornment.

Fourth, community engagement and dissensus necessitate an acceptance that some communities view display of their histories in museums (problematic as they may be) as markers of arrival and legitimization. For instance, some members of immigrant communities in the United States view the Smithsonian's "coverage" of their communities as a sign that they have been accepted and belong as "Americans" and thus are now part of the national narrative. Curators and collections must acknowledge and work with these beliefs as part of their collecting, record-making and label-writing processes. While curating *Beyond Bollywood*, I frequently encountered community members who wanted only successes and accomplishments of the community highlighted, to the exclusion of "dirty laundry" and struggles. These same community members revered the Hope Diamond and wanted artifacts of similar stature displayed in *Beyond Bollywood*, removed of any "troubling" or critical history.

Fifth, an activist view of collections puts repatriation and de-accessioning "on the table" as a part of any collections policy, along with loaning objects to community-based museums and local historical societies. Although many institutions don't want to let go of what they have, any number of "their" objects didn't belong to them in the first place and might have been initially acquired through theft, including the Hope Diamond. Moreover, some objects are in the wrong institutions and could be better valued and contextualized by other organizations.

Sixth, an activist view of collections prioritizes collecting, or at the very least helping to preserve, objects endangered in humanitarian crises, natural disasters, violent conflict and war, depending on the mission of the collecting institution. Although we'd like to have time to consider and collect all the objects that we encounter, this isn't always possible. So much of history and so many perspectives are lost during times of crisis, and institutions need to be able to respond flexibly through their collections policies and archival practices by collecting key objects related to crisis events.[3] Large museums in the Global North are currently working with communities and museum professionals in Iraq, Haiti and Syria to support such efforts.

Seventh, an activist approach to collections revisits canonical notions of what is "of value." If museums are no longer about encyclopedic collecting and supporting the grand narrative of European supremacy, we have to revisit how we assign value. For example, we need to question whether objects and material culture need to be the primary focus of collections. What about intangible cultural heritage, such as music and poetry? And what about digital media, including tweets and memes? However, in evaluating the role of material collections, we must take care not to equate civilized cultures with objects and marginalized communities with intangible cultural heritage.

Eighth, an activist approach to collections considers how digital tools and social media can help shift the balance of power and voice in museums by convening broader conversations around given objects and collections—and making these things more accessible. Online platforms allow more and more diverse visitors to engage with museum collections by learning about them, commenting on them and "remaking" interpretations of them. These platforms also allow museums to engage with audiences with whom they may not have a prior relationship or who cannot physically visit the museum.

Ninth, an activist approach to collections continuously questions whether something has to be collected and whether collected objects need to be saved versus repatriated, de-accessioned or disposed of. If we accept Merriman's assertion that museums are "partial, historically contingent, assemblages that reflect the tastes and interests of both the times and the individuals who made them" (2008, 3), we have to craft collections policies and approaches accordingly. Moreover, as Merriman points out, "today, the assumption that museum collections are physical embodiments of collective memory of the nation and are objective records through their tangibility and all-encompassing classificatory schemes is being questioned."

And tenth, an activist view of collections must be situated in the larger context of activist views/approaches to all of museum practice including curating, visitor engagement, education, marketing and communications, fundraising, and management. It's hard to expect an activist view of museum collections to survive if it is undermined by the larger context.

Revisiting the Hope Diamond, these ten principles imply a different interpretation of the object. How could the label be rewritten to reflect a multiplicity of perspective, including the associated glamour but also the colonialist provenance? Could research for this rewritten label be steeped in conversations with communities in India and the United States about repatriation? Could some of these conversations be convened digitally? Should the object itself be periodically replaced or moved to a different exhibit to provoke a conversation or cast it in a different light? Or, more provocatively, could it even be auctioned with proceeds going towards building a new gallery or exhibition more emblematic of the community? Such approaches would represent a new era for museum practitioners, both in their responsiveness to communities and their deliberately activist, anti-racist, anti-orientalist stances.

Notes

1 See, for example, the issues related to the Elgin or Parthenon Marbles, or the Nefertiti Bust.
2 For foundational discussions on knowledge as co-constructed, see Vygotsky (1978).
3 For an extensive discussion of this see Peterson (2012).

References

Alexander, Edward P., and Mary Alexander. 2008. *Museums in Motion: An Introduction to the History and Functions of Museums*. Plymouth, UK: AltaMira Press.
Conaty, Gerald T., ed. 2015. *We Are Coming Home: Repatriation and the Restoration of Blackfoot Cultural Confidence*. Toronto, Canada: Athabasca University Press.
Lynch, Bernadette T., and Samuel J.M.M. Alberti. 2010. "Legacies of Prejudice: Racism, Co-production and Radical Trust in the Museum." *Museum Management and Curatorship* 25(1): 13–35.

Merriman, Nick. 2008. "Museum Collections and Sustainability." *Cultural Trends* 17(1): 3–21.

Pearce, Susan. 1995. *On Collecting: An Investigation into Collecting in the European Tradition.* London: Routledge.

Peterson, Trudy Huskamp. 2012. "Human Rights, Human Wrongs, and Archives." *Revista Andaluza de Archivos* 5: 114–124.

Sandell, Richard, Annie Delin, Jocelyn Dodd, and Jackie Gay. 2005. "Beggars, Freaks and Heroes? Museums Collections and the Hidden History of Disability." *Museum Management and Curatorship* 20(1): 5–19.

Smithsonian Institution. 2003. "Encyclopedia Smithsonian: The Hope Diamond." http://www.si.edu/Encyclopedia_SI/nmnh/hope.htm.

Vygotsky, L.S. 1978. *Mind in Society: The Development of Higher Psychological Processes.* Cambridge, MA: Harvard University Press.

2

OBJECTS OR PEOPLE?

Rainey Tisdale

In "A Manifesto for Active History Museum Collections," one of the core statements Trevor Jones and I make is, "we need to change the conversation from caring for artifacts to caring about people" (Jones and Tisdale, this volume). We are certainly not the first to call for this shift in priorities, most notable among our antecedents being Stephen Weil's classic essay "From Being About Something to Being For Somebody" (Weil 1999). Despite field-wide support for Weil's argument, and those that have come after, most museums have had trouble putting this concept into practice, which is why it is still surfacing in the Active Collections Manifesto as unfinished business.

Unfinished business because admittedly it is easier said than done when the entire museum system continues to be organized around caring for artifacts. At a basic level, there is a calculus of proximal contact: the objects are under our roof every day, and we develop long-term relationships with them. We are trained to learn everything we can about them, to treat them like family. Meanwhile, the people come and go—we barely learn their names, let alone their provenance and preservation issues—and the ones who need us the most rarely cross the threshold. So, we keep starting with the objects ("We have this stuff; how can we get other people to care about it as much as we do?") instead of starting with people ("The communities we serve have needs; how could we use our stuff to address them?").

One of our goals as part of the Active Collections movement is to explore changes we could make to the museum system that would help us treat the people in our communities more like family, and care for them accordingly. The first step in achieving this goal is learning to understand the needs of people within a museum context as well as we understand the needs of objects. As museum workers we talk a lot about what objects need from their museum stewards: legal title, climate-controlled storage, security, housing, a number, a catalog record, conservation, research. What do people need from museums? Below I outline five pressing needs I see: the need for equity, the need for a healthier relationship with the material world, the need for a sustainable earth, the need to nurture our whole selves, and the need for poetry. With each of these needs, I pose new questions we might ask about the objects in our collections in order to reframe their value in relation to the people for whom we hold them in public trust.

People Need Equity

The #BlackLivesMatter movement has underscored how much systemic resistance there still is toward racial equity in this country. Meanwhile, in recent years it has been widely reported, based on historical U.S. Census and Internal Revenue Service data, that income inequality in the United States is at its highest point since the 1970s (Stone et al. 2015). And progress toward gender pay equity has more or less plateaued since 2001; women still make 78 cents to the male dollar (Council of Economic Advisers 2015).

Some museum workers may think that building a more equitable society is someone else's job, but we all share equally in both the rights and responsibilities of our membership in the human family. The work of building a more equitable society is everybody's work. It is museums' work. It is your work. It is my work. If anything, this work falls more heavily on institutions with a history of elitism and wealth accumulation (like museums) and with individuals who have benefitted from privilege (like me and the many other museum workers who are White and middle- or upper-class).

So what message does gallery after gallery filled with objects of power, framed through a lens of privilege—White objects, colonizing objects, male objects—send to people who don't share that privilege? What message do historic house museums send when 99% of them exclusively tell the story of the 1%? They say "this place is not for you." They sting and alienate—sometimes unconsciously and sometimes consciously—millions of people museums claim as members of our public audience. And yet museums keep insisting that the promises they made to previous generations of privileged people—promises to preserve the things that *they* thought were important—take precedence over the right to equality, respect, and welcome every human being deserves from a public institution in a democratic society.

This is not a new issue: inequity in museum collections has been a widespread topic for discussion—and sometimes action—throughout the field since the mid-twentieth century. For most American museums, the strategy for addressing this issue has been to acquire some objects that represent marginalized people here and there, wherever bursting storage facilities and meager resources would allow. These museums also have kept right on acquiring as many objects representing privilege as wealthy White families or collectors want to donate, without actively challenging museums' role in a larger social system that values White people's stuff, stories, and wealth accumulation over everyone else's (Kochhar and Fry 2014).[1] And where has that gotten us? Is it really any different than the jobs and schools and neighborhoods that were closed to all but a few token people of color until federal courts mandated otherwise? Indeed, is it going to take a museum version of affirmative action for our field to do something significant about this? If we zoom out past the way we have always done things to look at what our public audience truly needs from us, it may actually prove to be more—not less—ethical to deaccession and sell at auction a significant portion of the millions of objects of privilege currently held by museums, in order to free up resources and attention for collections that better serve the true breadth of that public audience.

My colleague Paul van de Laar at Rotterdam Museum makes the distinction between "nostalgia heritage" and "bonding heritage." Within the context of his work in Rotterdam, nostalgia heritage refers to collections and projects that reinforce the privilege of longtime residents of Dutch descent, who use history to remind themselves of the role their ancestors played in building the city. Looking back in this way makes them feel special, but it does so at the expense of others. "Bonding heritage," by contrast, is Van de Laar's term for collections and projects that make room for everyone—longtime Dutch residents as well as the scores of newcomers that are flocking to Rotterdam each year from all over the world. Bonding heritage recognizes that transnational newcomers care just as much about the city—they want to know it, find their place in it, and put down roots—but the conventional version of Rotterdam's history, framed through the lens of privilege, at best holds little meaning for them and at worst excludes them (Van de Laar 2013). If we expand Van de Laar's bonding heritage to consider all the different ways inclusion and exclusion can be parsed—ability, sexual and gender orientation, politics, religion, and more—we can begin to see the possibility of collections that nurture an equitable common ground instead of collections that reinforce a hierarchy of privilege.

If the people museums serve need and deserve equity, what kind of questions might we ask of objects when we are making decisions about acquisition, preservation, use, and deaccession?

- Does this object—or its presentation—reinforce a system of inequality, colonialism, or privilege?
- Are we using this object for bonding or nostalgia?
- Are decisions about what we take and keep made exclusively by people of privilege?
- Is the presence of this object in our collection worth alienating another human being, or undermining another human being's value?
- How might we use this object to reinforce a system of equity, welcome, and mutual respect?

People Need a Healthy Relationship with the Material World

The majority of twenty-first-century Americans are drowning in material goods. There is a large body of social science research showing how detrimental hyperconsumerism has become. A 2007 comprehensive study of 30 middle-class families in Los Angeles, documented in the fascinating book *Life at Home in the 21st Century*, details in high relief an all too familiar reality experienced across the United States in which families find themselves caught in a vicious cycle of "escalating consumerism, increasing time spent at work, growing heaps of possessions at home, rising stress, and declining leisure" (Arnold 2013, 71). The same study found a relationship between the amount of clutter in a home and the levels of both cortisol (a stress hormone) and depression documented in the adult female participants (Saxbe and Repetti 2010).

Meanwhile, in *The High Price of Materialism*, psychologist Tim Kasser summarizes decades of research in his own lab and by others in the United States and around the globe regarding the negative effects of materialism—the pursuit of wealth and possessions—concluding, "strong materialistic values are associated with a pervasive undermining of people's well-being, from low life satisfaction and happiness, to depression and anxiety, to physical problems such as headaches, and to personality disorders, narcissism, and antisocial behavior" (Kasser 2003, 22). And in 2014, Havas Worldwide commissioned a survey across 29 countries, finding that 69% of respondents felt "over-consumption is putting our society and the planet at risk," with 52% reporting, "I could happily live without most of the items I own." The report concludes that on a global scale, "consumption has become a chore and an emotional burden" (Havas Worldwide 2014). While hyper-consumerism in many ways is a mark of socioeconomic status (one has to have disposable income in order to accumulate a lot of stuff), it is affecting lower and lower rungs of the socioeconomic ladder due to the increasing availability of cheap goods. Moreover, a continued emphasis on materialism, and the social expectations it creates, has an impact on all socioeconomic levels by valuing those who consume and accumulate more than those who do not. In small ways and big ways, on an individual level and on a collective level, hyper-consumerism is exacting a toll on human beings.

Museums are not neutral on this issue. As caretakers of stuff—lots of stuff—it behooves the museum field to ask, amidst all this hyper-consumerism, whether we are helping or hurting the situation. A hundred years ago during a time of significantly less material saturation, collections philosophies like "keep acquiring—the bigger the collection, the better" and "collect comprehensively—at least one of everything, and one of each updated model too" made sense. But as Benjamin Filene argues elsewhere in this volume, these are different times. We now understand that comprehensive collections are no longer a realistic goal; after the twentieth century's floodgates of mass production it is simply impossible. Moreover, it is not just that it cannot be done; the social science research suggests it would not serve twenty-first-century humans to do so. More stuff is no longer better; in fact in many cases it is actually worse.

While hyper-consumerism is a concern behind the scenes in collections stewardship decisions, it is also a concern in terms of how collections are interpreted and displayed. Since the cabinet of curiosities days, museums have relied on the evocation of abundance as one of the most reliable tools in their toolkit. Visitors enter a gallery packed to the gills with objects in all their rich and varied colors and textures, and they are flooded with an intense feeling of material satiation—like a sugar rush. That feeling might have been rare and special a hundred years ago, but now most of us are getting a constant stream of it every day, everywhere we turn. Supermarkets and big box stores brimming with stuff. Homes and offices piled with stuff on every available surface. The majority of Americans don't need more abundance. It is highly likely that what they need now from museums are simple, calming spaces with plenty of room to move and breathe, where authenticity and quality (narrative, functional, or aesthetic) trump quantity. And they need help learning how to develop healthier relationships with objects outside the museum, in their everyday lives.

Some big thinkers have been exploring the ways taming hyper-consumerism need not be just a turning away from, but can also be a turning toward. In his article "Materialism and the Evolution of Consciousness," the sociologist Mihalyi Csikszentmihalyi explains the difference between *pleasurable* activities that satisfy our basic survival needs (eating, resting, sex) and *enjoyable* activities that lead to a less tangible, higher order satisfaction of self-actualization (mastering skills, meeting challenges, creative acts). Because material possessions are associated with creature comfort, acquiring them is a pleasurable activity (so is watching TV). Humans are wired to be easily seduced by pleasurable activities because they feed our basic survival instincts in the short term, but Csikszentmihalyi's (and other's) research suggests it is the enjoyable activities that make us healthier and happier over a lifetime. A mindful turning away from hyper-consumerism, therefore, can be a turning toward enjoyable and transformative personal growth (Csikszentmihalyi 2003). Meanwhile the economist Juliet Schor maps out an alternative model where the time we all currently spend working to support our hyper-consumptive lifestyles could be reallocated toward a more diversified and sustainable system. In her economic model, we practice *true materialism*: "We don't need to be less materialist, as the standard formulation would have it, but more so. For it is only when we take the materiality of the world seriously that we can appreciate and preserve the resources on which spending depends" (Schor 2010, 6). True materialism means fully appreciating each object and the spectrum of resources required to produce it, such that we choose to surround ourselves with fewer objects, but each one ethically and sustainably made and offering deeper meaning, functionality, or beauty.

If humans need and deserve a healthier relationship with the material world, how might museums help them put that need into practice, and accordingly, what kind of questions might we ask of objects when we are making decisions about acquisition, preservation, use, and deaccession?

- Does our museum have a healthy relationship with stuff?
- Would this object belong in a "just enough"-sized collection or a "more is better"-sized collection?
- Is this object worth a reduction in mental and physical well-being—in our public audience and in our museum workers? Does it send a message that humans are only valued in relation to their buying power?
- How might we use our collection to model and teach "true materialism"?

People Need a Sustainable Earth

At this point the precarious situation of our planet is well known and documented: climate change, massive deforestation and other dwindling natural resources, thousands of species facing extinction, water and food instability, extreme weather. What is less clear is whether we—each of us members of the human family and residents of planet Earth—will come together to right this situation before it is too late.

In the same way that the price of a product on the shelf of a supermarket or shopping mall does not reflect the true cost of the resources required to make it, the price of preserving each object in a museum collection does not yet include the carbon footprint required for its maintenance. Each decision to acquire, keep, exhibit, or loan an object does indeed carry an environmental cost, and under the conventional standards of collections care, the cost can be great. Galleries and collections storage areas require 24/7 HVAC systems that maintain a constant temperature and humidity set point regardless of the weather outside. Each object needs archival-quality housing—boxes, bags, sleeves, padding. Museum loans present a particularly significant carbon footprint, as they often require special packing materials, crates, shipping arrangements, and couriers. The conventional standards were developed during a time of relative abundance, before our awareness of climate change reached its current undeniable level. The signs are clear all around us that we must rethink these standards now. What does it matter whether museums preserve the world's heritage for future generations if life on Earth becomes so unstable that there are no more future generations left?

During the last decade, symposia to explore the relationship between museum collections and climate change have been organized by preservation leaders such as the International Institute for Conservation, the Getty Conservation Institute, and the National Endowment for the Humanities. As a result, some of the organizations that produce guidelines for collections care—the Canadian Conservation Institute and the American Institute for Conservation among them—have revisited their long-held standards for artifact storage of 50% +/−5% relative humidity and 70 degrees +/−2, advising that most objects could withstand broader parameters in the interest of greater HVAC efficiency (Grattan and Michalski 2015; "Environmental Guidelines" 2014). Some professional associations, most notably the UK Museums Association, have worked to develop resources for member museums on measuring and reducing their carbon footprints. And Simon Lambert and Jane Henderson in the Department of Archaeology and Conservation at Cardiff University have developed a tool for calculating the carbon footprint of museum loans, using National Museum Wales as a case study (Lambert and Henderson 2011).

Certainly these are useful steps. But when the stakes are this high, we have a responsibility—as institutions that serve the public interest—to go beyond mere incremental greening of our current practices to re-evaluate holistically our underlying collections stewardship values in light of climate change. In a presentation at the Sustainable Cultural Heritage conference held in Washington, DC, in 2009, Gerry Podany, then Senior Conservator of Antiquities at the J. Paul Getty

Museum, argued, "It is time for us to ask what we really need, what our collections really need, versus what we have come to think is ideal and what we think we can provide . . . or once could provide, seemingly free of consequences and in a world of cheap and ample energy" (Podany 2009, 7). Indeed, what is truly essential? Up until now we have been assuming that all of our objects are worth their carbon footprint; probably some are and some are not. We have also been assuming that climate change should not have any bearing on the rate at which we acquire new objects for the collection; maybe it should. And maybe carbon offsetting is a responsible and ethical way to spend funds from the sale of deaccessioned artifacts.

If people need and deserve museums that pull their full weight in the transition to a sustainable society, and model responsible resource stewardship to their communities, what kind of questions might we ask of objects when we are making decisions about acquisition, preservation, use, and deaccession?

- Instead of how big a collection would we *like*, how big a collection do we *need*?
- Is this object (or this loan or traveling exhibition) worth its carbon footprint?
- Could this object better serve society if it were deaccessioned and then reused or recycled in a way that would reduce current fossil fuel dependency?
- How might we use this object to explore or model sustainable living?

People Need Attention to the Whole Self

In our 2013 book *Creativity in Museums*, Linda Norris and I argued that we have been moving from an industrial economy to a service economy to a creative economy—indeed a creative society—and that museums are uniquely positioned to develop the creative thinking skills people today need to thrive in a world with a lot less straight paths and clear guidelines (Norris and Tisdale 2013). I still stand by that argument, but I have come to see that it is not just creativity that is needed to prepare us for the complexity and challenges of the twenty-first century; it's bigger than that. What we need now is for people to apply everything they've got—their knowledge and skills but also their passion, their empathy, their spirituality, their human vulnerability, their commitment to the greater good—and yes, creativity—to help solve the entrenched, complex problems of our global society: the problems I mention above as well as countless others. In other words, we need people to bring their whole selves to the twenty-first-century table.

Exploring the role museums might play in helping people develop their "whole selves" involves first understanding what that term means. For the most part, the field of psychology has rejected the notion of a whole or integrated self. Particularly after the influence of postmodernism, most psychologists have argued that humans—our states of consciousness, our identities, our ways of operating in the world—are too fragmented and shifting to ever be some integrated whole that we can call the self. Yet this concept of the "whole self" keeps coming up in everyday language as something humans need and value, nonetheless.

There is one branch of psychology—humanistic psychology—that does grapple with the notion of the whole self. Starting in the 1960s, humanistic psychologists asserted that each of us is a whole that is greater than the sum of its parts, and that each of us is always in the process of developing and becoming. In this sense, we might say that the whole self is not something we ever attain, but nonetheless it is the thing we are always striving for, and the closer we get to it—or in those brief moments where we feel whole before we fragment again—the more alive, self-actualized, and high-functioning we feel. While there is more research to be done, the field of neuroscience, by observing which areas of the brain are activated for different processes, is beginning to support the idea that humans are indeed wholes greater than the sum of our parts—complex systems that are highly dynamic, inter-dependent, and contextual (DeRobertis 2014; Kuhl et al. 2015).

Often we think of the key parts of the self as mind, body, and spirit. For the museum field's purposes, I want to put forward a framework of the unique self's nine spheres of operation in the world: the learning self, the embodied self, the feeling self, the social self, the creative self, the civic self, the spiritual self, the playful self, and the vulnerable self. This framework shares similarities with Jan Packer and Roy Ballantyne's model of the ten facets of visitor experience: physical, sensory, restorative, introspective, transformative, hedonic, emotional, relational, spiritual, and cognitive (Packer and Ballantyne 2016). It also relates to Kiersten F. Latham's concept, in describing elements of numinous museum experiences, of "*Unity of the Moment,* the total holistic and dynamic experience" where everything—"emotion, intellect, feeling, senses, imagination"—comes together for the visitor in a unifying burst of clarity (Latham 2013, 8–11). In many of our social institutions, these spheres of operation are compartmentalized: you bring your learning self to school, your bodily self to the doctor's office, your spiritual self to a place of worship. I am arguing that because of our flexible, informal, and immersive environments, museums are positioned to attend to the whole self in a way that other social institutions cannot. We can deploy our resources—our collections, our buildings, our programming—to create opportunities for what we might call not just free choice learning but free choice development of the whole self.

As a field we have started to recognize how these nine spheres of operation might work together within a museum context for our public audiences. For example, there is broad consensus in museum pedagogy about the role the embodied self, the feeling self, and the social self play in learning. Researchers in Switzerland have been attaching physiological and motion sensors to art museum visitors to understand how "embodied cognition": the correlation between the bodily, spatial, and emotional experiences—of the artwork, the gallery space, and the interpretive methods—influences not just learning but also the aesthetic experience of artwork (Tröndle and Tschacher 2012). Jan Packer and Nigel Bond are studying the ways that museums serve as restorative environments for the vulnerable self (Packer and Bond 2010). My own work with Linda Norris has explored how creativity boosts self-actualization when it is combined with any of the other spheres of operation, and how play in turn boosts creativity. If we continue to study and experiment with methods for integrating these parts of the self we might find that, all along, the phenomenon we have ultimately been trying to produce in visitors—whatever we choose to call it: unity of the moment, peak experience, aha moment—is one of briefly being whole. And if so, then it would be useful to consider how our collections could better contribute to whole-self experiences.

As a concrete example, let's consider the Rubin Museum's Dream-Over program, which invites members of the public to spend a night at the museum, dreaming about an object in the collection. Participants fill out a questionnaire that helps museum staff match them to one of the artifacts on display. During the event, participants draw their objects; listen to bedtime stories chosen especially for them; learn contextual information about dreaming, their artwork, and Buddhist culture; and sleep next to their object overnight. In the morning a team of psychoanalysts help them capture their dreams, and small group discussions help participants process them (Hiebert 2011). This program integrates the embodied, feeling, social, spiritual, creative, playful, learning, and vulnerable selves for a rich and personal experience, such that the program repeatedly sells out. Imagine how else we might increase the value of museum collections for the people we serve—and for society as a whole—if we actively and intentionally consider objects' potential to address not just learning but also other human needs: healing, self-reflection, social bridging, activism, idea generation. Perhaps we might even find ways to more fully attend to *museum workers'* whole selves in the process.

If humans need and deserve collections that support whole-self development, what kind of questions might we ask of objects when we are making decisions about acquisition, preservation, use, and deaccession?

- How might this object be a tool for the whole self—to feed and restore the body or the heart; to inspire conscientious civic engagement; to encourage social bonding and bridging, play, creativity, or spiritual reflection?
- What is this object's potential to be a prescription? A touchstone? A divining rod? A lightbulb?
- Do our museum methods—the collections database; the acquisition, research, and exhibition development processes—allow for holistic exploration of our collection, or do they favor the cognitive self above all other spheres of operation?

People Need Poetry

The ecologist Betsy MacWhinney published an essay in the *New York Times* in 2015 about her experience trying to single-parent a teenage daughter while that teenage daughter's world was falling apart. Desperately grasping for ways to keep her daughter in the land of the living, she took to printing out poems—Theodore Roethke, Wendell Berry—to leave in her daughter's shoes. She explained that she wanted her daughter to understand "the thoughts of others who struggled to make a meaningful life and had put those thoughts into the best, sparest words they could." And then she goes on to say, "It suddenly struck me—I the one who loves science, data, facts and reason—that when push comes to shove, it was poetry I could count on. Poetry knew where hope lived and could elicit that lump in the throat that reminds me it's all worth it. Science couldn't do that" (MacWhinney 2015). When it does its job, poetry does indeed produce that lump in the throat, that moment when everything suddenly comes into focus and you see your place in the universe.

In her essay "The Poetry of the Museum," Kiersten F. Latham takes theories about reading text and applies them to museum experiences. She describes a continuum of visitor experiences with objects: on one end of the continuum is the *efferent* experience, where the visitor accesses bits of information about an object—in text terms this is like reading a recipe or an instruction manual. On the other end of the continuum is a *transcendent or aesthetic* experience of an object—one that involves not just information but emotion and reflection. This second kind—the transcendent experience—is the thing that happens when you read a profound and moving poem. Indeed, Latham's overall point is that when museums are at their best they make poetry (Latham 2007). The aha moment or the peak experience is not just a moment of self-integration; it is also a moment of poetry. Not poetry in the sense of rarified high culture, but poetry in the sense of human meaning beautifully distilled into its most concentrated form.

Historically, much of the practice of museums, and museum collections, has revolved around the desire to be three-dimensional encyclopedias, presenting the world's heritage in a classified and chronological order, always striving to be comprehensive and fill in the gaps. Even as some museums have moved away from this encyclopedic notion, its legacy still remains in the ways our collections stewardship model favors comprehensive or complete collections as an ultimate goal. But, as discussed above, museum collections have never been, nor will they ever be, encyclopedic or comprehensive—we have always left out much more than we have saved, like encyclopedias with half the pages missing. What's more, most of us now carry around a much more powerful encyclopedia in our pockets, liberating all but a few key museums from the need to even attempt this function. But there is a kind of "text" that people still deeply need from museums: poetry.

From systemic inequality to climate change to economic insecurity to global migration to political polarization to the enormous disruption to personal and work life brought about by the Information Revolution, twenty-first-century people are starving for enlightenment and grounding, for reassurance that generations and generations of humans have struggled through just as much and survived, and for the inspiration they need to keep trying and reaching. Mary Oliver writes that "Poems are not words, after all, but fires for the cold, ropes let down to the lost, something as necessary as bread in the pockets of the hungry" (Oliver 1994, 122). In this time of tremendous upheaval, people need as much poetry as they can get their hands on. That is a powerful vision for what our collections—and our museums—can be for the people we serve.

Poets carefully choose words for maximum effect and maximum meaning. We could call this process a form of "word stewardship": which words to keep, which words to let go of, which new words to acquire. Unlike the academic paper (or many museum labels), a hallmark of poetry is its economy: poets don't put every word they can on the page; instead they seek out the most interesting or compelling words and combine them in surprising and powerful ways: human meaning beautifully distilled into its most concentrated form. We don't expect a poem to be comprehensive. Therefore, a poet's process of *word* discernment and economy can serve as inspiration for a museum process of *object* discernment and economy: not just any object we can, but the objects that best help our visitors move toward equity and true materialism, the objects that best equip our visitors to ask bigger questions of the world, the objects that best inspire and fortify them to be engaged citizens, the objects that best speak to their whole selves. By releasing ourselves from the expectation that museums should be encyclopedic and instead choosing poetry as our model, we pave the way for leaner collections with greater impact.

If humans need and deserve poetic museums, what kind of questions might we ask of objects when we are making decisions about acquisition, preservation, use, and deaccession?

- How concentrated is human meaning in this object?
- Is this object here merely because it is the best thing we have found so far to fill a gap in the encyclopedia, or is it here because it has poetic possibility?
- How might we share our collection poetically, seeking out the most interesting or compelling objects and combining them in surprising and powerful ways?
- What might the poetic version of a collecting scope be for our museum?

Conclusion

We museum workers often get caught up in thinking that preserving objects is filling a pressing community need. It's not. As Stephen Weil himself argues, preservation, interpretation, and scholarship are not in and of themselves public services. They are merely the means to an end, where the "end" is direct impact on human lives and communities. As Weil sees it, each generation has different needs, and as these needs change, museums' "most important new skill will be the ability to envision how the community's ongoing and/or emerging needs in all their dimensions—physical, psychological, economic, and social—might be served by the museum's particular competencies" (Weil 1999, 253).

And this is the larger point: museums aren't just neutral entities doing their work in a vacuum but instead are actors in a larger social and political system. When we treat museum objects—and the stewardship practices that govern them—as inherently valuable, immutable, and sacred, we are ill-equipped to recognize the instances where they have become relatively valueless in a changing social and political system. Then we become ill-equipped to respond to the changing needs of the people we serve. Yet everything does continue to change around us.

And people continue to need. The Latin root of the word "curate" is *curare*, to care. In early usage, it referred to caring for people—not objects—in a religious or government role. So objects or people? Objects in the service of people. That is what it means for museums to hold their collections in the public trust.

Note

1 Based on data from the Federal Reserve's Survey of Consumer Finances, White families in the United States hold 13 times the wealth of Black families and 10 times the wealth of Hispanic families.

References

Arnold, Jeanne E. 2013. "Mountains of Things." In *Fast-Forward Family: Home, Work, and Relationships in Middle-Class America*, edited by Elinor Ochs and Tamar Kremer-Sadlik, 67–93. Berkeley: University of California Press.

Council of Economic Advisers. 2015. "Gender Pay Gap: Recent Trends and Explanations." Issues Brief. Washington, DC: The White House. https://www.whitehouse.gov/sites/default/files/docs/equal_pay_issue_brief_final.pdf.

Csikszentmihalyi, Mihaly. 2003. "Materialism and the Evolution of Consciousness." In *Psychology and Consumer Culture*, edited by Tim Kasser and Allen Kanner, 91–106. Washington, DC: American Psychological Association.

DeRobertis, Eugene M. 2014. "A Neuroscientific Renaissance of Humanistic Psychology." *Journal of Humanistic Psychology* 55(3): 323–345.

"Environmental Guidelines." 2014. *AIC Wiki, American Institute for Conservation*. July 24. http://www.conservation-wiki.com/w/index.php?title=Environmental_Guidelines.

Grattan, David, and Stefan Michalski. 2015. "Environmental Guidelines for Museums." Canadian Conservation Institute. http://canada.pch.gc.ca/eng/1444920450420.

Havas Worldwide. 2014. "The New Consumer and the Sharing Economy." 18. Prosumer Reports. Havas Worldwide. http://mag.havasww.com/prosumer-report/the-new-consumer-and-the-sharing-economy/.

Hiebert, Paul. 2011. "A Night at the Museum: The Rubin's 'Dream-Over' in Photos." Flavorwire. March 8. http://flavorwire.com/157675/a-night-at-the-museum-the-rubins-dream-over-in-photos/.

Kasser, Tim. 2003. *The High Price of Materialism*. Cambridge, MA: MIT Press.

Kochhar, Rakesh, and Richard Fry. 2014. "Wealth Inequality has Widened along Racial, Ethnic Lines since End of Great Recession." *FactTank*, Pew Research Center. December 12. http://www.pewresearch.org/fact-tank/2014/12/12/racial-wealth-gaps-great-recession/.

Kuhl, Julius, Markus Quirin, and Sander L. Koole. 2015. "Being Someone: The Integrated Self as a Neuropsychological System." *Social and Personality Psychology Compass* 9(3): 115–132. doi:10.1111/spc3.12162.

Lambert, Simon, and Jane Henderson. 2011. "The Carbon Footprint of Museum Loans: A Pilot Study at Amgueddfa Cymru—National Museum Wales." *Museum Management and Curatorship* 26(3): 1–27.

Latham, Kiersten F. 2007. "The Poetry of the Museum: A Holistic Model of Numinous Museum Experiences." *Museum Management and Curatorship* 22(3): 247–263. doi:10.1080/09647770701628594.

———. 2013. "Numinous Experiences with Museum Objects." *Visitor Studies* 16(1): 3–20. doi:10.1080/10645578.2013.767728.

MacWhinney, Betsy. 2015. "Bringing a Daughter Back from the Brink with Poems." *New York Times*. February 26. http://www.nytimes.com/2015/03/01/style/bringing-a-daughter-back-from-the-brink-with-poems.html.

Norris, Linda, and Rainey Tisdale. 2013. *Creativity in Museum Practice*. Walnut Creek, CA: Routledge.

Oliver, Mary. 1994. *A Poetry Handbook*. 1 edition. San Diego, CA: Mariner Books.

Packer, Jan, and Roy Ballantyne. 2016. "Conceptualizing the Visitor Experience: A Review of Literature and Development of a Multifaceted Model." *Visitor Studies* 19(2): 128–143. doi:10.1080/10645578.2016.1144023.

Packer, Jan, and Nigel Bond. 2010. "Museums as Restorative Environments." *Curator: The Museum Journal* 53(4): 421–436. doi:10.1111/j.2151-6952.2010.00044.x.

Podany, Jerry. 2009. "Sustainable Stewardship: Preventative Conservation in a Changing World." Washington, DC: National Endowment for the Humanities. http://www.neh.gov/files/divisions/preservation/podany.pdf.

Saxbe, Darby E., and Rena Repetti. 2010. "No Place Like Home: Home Tours Correlate With Daily Patterns of Mood and Cortisol." *Personality and Social Psychology Bulletin* 36(1): 71–81. doi:10.1177/0146167209352864.

Schor, Juliet B. 2010. *Plenitude*. New York: The Penguin Press.

Stone, Chad, Danilo Trisi, Arloc Sherman, and Brandon DeBot. 2015. "A Guide to Statistics on Historical Trends in Income Inequality." Washington, DC: Center on Budget and Policy Priorities. http://www.cbpp.org/sites/default/files/atoms/files/11-28-11pov_0.pdf.

Tröndle, Martin, and Wolfgang Tschacher. 2012. "The Physiology of Phenomenology: The Effects of Artworks." *Empirical Studies of the Arts* 30(1): 75–113. doi:10.2190/EM.30.1.g.

Van de Laar, Paul. 2013. "The Contemporary City as Backbone: Museum Rotterdam Meets the Challenge." *Journal of Museum Education* 38(1): 39–49.

Weil, Stephen E. 1999. "From Being about Something to Being for Somebody: The Ongoing Transformation of the American Museum." *Daedalus* 128(3): 229–258.

SENSORY DEPRIVATION

A Short Play Based on a Real-Life Scenario

Elizabeth Wood

Cast:
Active Collections Advocate
History Curator, interested in new collections practices

Setting:
Discussing an exhibition project in the last stages before opening

HISTORY CURATOR (HC): Hey, the suit of armor just came in—it is absolutely gorgeous!

ACTIVE COLLECTIONS ADVOCATE (ACA): That's great! I'm sure you are in heaven—didn't you study that in college?

HC: That and military history in general. This suit is just so fantastic, it is actually my size. I was so dying to try it on. I just want to know what it feels like.

ACA: AH! Cool—*did* you try it on?

HC: NO!

ACA: Oh come on, why not?

HC: Well it's a collections object for one.

ACA: And it's metal . . .

HC: And that would just be wrong. What if I damaged it?

ACA: Of all the people in this museum YOU are the best person to handle it. You've done all this research on it, you know how to properly work with the object. Why wouldn't you want to see what it was like?

HC: But, you, but . . .

ACA: Wouldn't it be worth someone actually having first-hand knowledge to help visitors know what it is like to wear it?

HC: Oh, well, yes, but . . .

ACA: But what? You have the knowledge, the skill and expertise and the capacity to do it. So why wouldn't you?

HC: Collections policy! Best practices? Uh . . . I . . . because it goes against everything I was trained for. I just couldn't.

ACA: . . . that's too bad . . . all the things we will never know.

HC: Don't tempt me more . . . Oh geez.

END

Would you wear the suit of armor? Why or why not?

3

MUSEUM COLLECTIONS AND PUBLIC FEELINGS

Modupe Labode

Creative, forward-thinking museum practitioners are exploring the many facets of emotions associated with objects in collections. Museum professionals and those based in the academy are raising provocative questions about the emotional life of objects in the museum, the empathetic museum, the "museum effect," and how visitors make emotional connections to collection items (Besley 2014; Edwards 2010; The Empathetic Museum 2016; Rose 2005; Wood and Latham 2014). This essay suggests adding the concept of public feelings to this ongoing exploration of emotions in museums. Public feelings are complex emotions expressed in public or semi-public spaces that emerge in response to social, political, and economic events or factors. This concept offers an additional way to understand and capture the emotional resonance of items in museum collections, and, by extension, an additional way to understand if and how objects are truly active and useful. Because public feelings are often an important part of how museum objects have been used over time, I suggest that the emotional contexts associated with an object should be documented and made accessible to those who engage with the object, whether members of the public or museum professionals.

In the early twenty-first century, a loose coalition of scholars and activists came together to discuss the public meaning of their emotional states and developed the concept of "public feelings." Literature scholar Ann Cvetkovich notes that this concept emerged in a political context, as activists felt pulled between their feelings and norms of political behavior that minimize or discount emotional responses to injustice and political activism. Cvetkovich (2012) states that the idea of public feelings is indebted to African American studies, feminist thought, and queer theory, all areas of inquiry that take seriously complex feelings and states of mind, such as exhaustion, melancholy, shame, rage, self-doubt, and joy. For example, the feelings that emerge when one is on a protest march—rage or indignation at an injustice, apprehension of criticism, anticipatory fear of opposition, elation at experiencing camaraderie—are not inherently separate from the issue that one is protesting. Proponents of public feelings argue that accepting sentiment, sensibility, and feelings as legitimate responses to events in public life does not imply that people are "wallowing" in emotion or that sentiment should be the ultimate response to injustice. Further, public feelings are not universal, as not all groups or communities experience the same sentiments. Different groups of people may experience different public feelings in relation to the same event as it is unfolding, and then still other public feelings may emerge toward that event over time as its meaning becomes subject to historical interpretation. Because public feelings are products of specific cultural, historical, political, and economic forces (Jackson and Meiners 2011), accounting for the larger context in which they emerge or are expressed is essential.

Erika Doss, in her study of contemporary memorials, uses the concept of public feelings to understand the ways Americans commemorate historical events in the late twentieth and early twenty-first centuries. In previous decades, communities dedicated monuments to leaders whose public actions or characteristics were admirable. Today's monuments, Doss argues, often are public manifestations of complex emotional states. For example, monuments to fallen veterans embody a community's expressions of grief and gratitude, and the specific war or military action may be secondary considerations. A monument in Duluth, Minnesota, honors three African American men—Elias Clayton, Elmer Jackson, and Isaac McGhie—who were murdered by a lynch mob in 1920. The monument also provides a focal point for community members' feelings of shame, regret, anger, and desire to apologize. Importantly, the creation of the monument and the annual "Day of Remembrance" ceremony are touchstones for those who wish to atone for the previous injustice and are also committed to confronting contemporary racism (Doss 2010, 265–286; Passi 2016).

Jessi Lee Jackson and Erica Meiners (2011) argue that the public feelings of groups with privilege and power, rarely acknowledged directly but nonetheless very much present as a subtext to political discourse, underpin public policy in relationship to criminal justice and incarceration. In their analysis, complex feelings of pity, fear, anger, and disgust fuel the political actions by groups that have both shaped public ideas about criminality and punitive approaches to criminal justice since the 1960s in the United States. In order to change policy and effect a change in the public's attitudes about mass incarceration, Jackson and Meiners suggest that activists call attention to the ways these feelings contribute to ideas of "public safety," bring these feelings to the surface, and propose alternative approaches to the concept of "safe" communities.

The scholarship of public feelings, coming from diverse fields, provides examples for those working in museums. Attention to public feelings may provide a way to animate objects by revealing unquestioned assumptions about material culture, bringing hidden meanings to the surface, or proposing alternative interpretations of an object's significance. Public feelings are rarely single or straightforward; therefore, it is important that museums resist the urge to simplify complex public feelings, given museums' ongoing difficulty with accounting for multiple, diverse perspectives, not only with respect to staff or audience, but also with respect to objects. When museum professionals use objects in programs, research, or exhibitions, they need to be aware of what writer Chimamanda Ngozi Adichie calls "the danger of a single story." She notes that, "The single story creates stereotypes, and the problem with stereotypes is not that they are untrue, but that they are incomplete. They make one story become the only story" (Adichie 2009). The power of collecting multiple sentiments around mundane objects is illustrated in Eula Biss's essay on the telephone pole. Biss writes that as telephone poles populated the landscape from the late 1800s, Americans interpreted these objects as symbols of modernity or destruction of a simpler way of life (Biss 2009). But telephone poles also were tools of lynching, as an untold number of White supremacist crowds killed African Americans by hanging them from telephone poles. Biss suggests that Americans should keep all the meanings of telephone poles in their minds, and not attempt to evade or deflect the public feelings elicited by this object's association with lynching.

Museums are filled with objects about which they are telling only a single story. The observations of Adichie and Biss remind us, however, that choosing to tell a single story is, at best, misleading. So, for example, if a museum uses an object like a spike maul (a tool to hammer railroad ties) to call forth a conventional, monolithic narrative of building the United States' transcontinental railroad without also calling attention to Americans for whom that same tool signifies the labor of Chinese workers, the violent displacement of indigenous people, or the opportunity railroad labor provided European immigrants, it becomes a single story instead of a more nuanced, multifaceted one. Public feelings are by definition about multiplicity, and recognizing the public feelings associated with objects, and how they change based on context, may help counter museum professionals' tendency to use an object to tell a single story, introducing opportunities for complexity and empathy in the process.

Two short thought experiments indicate how public feelings could activate museum collections to tell more complex and compelling stories. These experiments begin with brief historical sketches that provide the context for the object, and then consider the issues that the historical précis raises. The first thought experiment concerns the Mother Hubbard, a simple style of women's dress that became popular in the United States during the nineteenth century. The second experiment concerns household and decorative objects made from elephant ivory. These examples reflect the ordinary type of objects that fill many museums. While many museum professionals find it easier to tell stories about unusual or iconic objects, more mundane museum objects languish unused, in part because their ordinariness appears to preclude active, new stories. In these examples, the history of the objects and the public feelings associated open new interpretive possibilities.

The Mother Hubbard Dress

The Mother Hubbard was not stylish, but was easy to make and easy to wear. In the United States, women started wearing these dresses, named for the nursery rhyme character, after the Civil War. The Mother Hubbard was usually made from inexpensive cotton material, hung loosely from the shoulders to the ankles and sometimes opened at the front. The Mother Hubbard allowed pregnant women and those doing heavy work at home or on the farm to be comfortable and move easily. Missionaries from the United States and Europe introduced this style of dress to indigenous women converts, especially when they judged the women's traditional clothing to be immodest (Marks 2016, 299). Despite the missionaries' biased assumptions, women in North America, sub-Saharan Africa, and the Pacific adopted the dress and made it their own (Gray 2014, 59–63) (Figure 3.1). Women throughout the Pacific Islands altered the western style by using local materials, for example constructing a Mother Hubbard dress from traditional barkcloth, with a hibiscus fringe as decoration (Te Papa Museum 2003). In Arctic regions of North America, indigenous women in some communities adapted the Mother Hubbard to the parka, adding a ruffle and calico shell over (or sometimes under) a wool or fur-lined coat (Winnipeg Art Gallery 2002).

While the Mother Hubbard was acceptable dress for women to wear at home, in the United States, the dress, when worn by women in public or on the street

FIGURE 3.1   Tahitian Girls Wearing Mother Hubbard Dress. Unknown [Public domain], via Wikimedia Commons. Paris: Photothèque du Musée de l'Homme, 1880–1889

became a focal point for public feelings about gender, class, race, and location. As Patricia Marks notes, in urban areas, only "children and prostitutes wore the dress outdoors . . . [the Mother Hubbard] clearly defined not only social class but moral status" (2016, 299). By the early twentieth century, women who wore this garment were seen to be poor, uncouth, and possibly immoral and so the public feelings associated with the Mother Hubbard began to include censoriousness, condemnation, and shame. In Agnes Smedley's 1929 novel *Daughter of the Earth*, the protagonist describes her grandmother as a "tall, strong woman" who "went barefoot, smoked a corn-cob pipe, and wore loose, flowing Mother Hubbards" (17–18). The grandmother's dress marked both her rural poverty and the hill culture of turn-of-the-century Missouri.

Around the time of World War I, some respectable African American women in Detroit tried to convince new migrants from the South to stop wearing the Mother Hubbard in public, because in their eyes it was a marker of both rural backwardness and sexual immorality (Wolcott 2001, 56–58). The critics, acutely attuned to how Whites viewed all African Americans, complained that these new arrivals gave Whites a bad impression of the entire race, thus providing an excuse to impose racial segregation. This sharp critique of southern women migrants to the city carries with it a sense of racial self-consciousness, perhaps because in the eyes of Whites, the association between prostitution and the Mother Hubbard impugned the sexual morality of all Black women. To be clear, the clothing or behavior of southern African Americans did not cause the widespread racial discrimination and segregation in northern cities. The public feelings of the women who wore the Mother Hubbard in public, however, are more difficult to discern. Employing historical empathy, we might consider whether these women perhaps saw their clothing as a connection to their rural background and an implicit rejection of the authority of those who badgered them to adapt to urban life.

By contrast, in other areas of the world, the dress became associated with resilient and adaptable indigenous culture (Cummings 2013). For example, a cotton *mu'umu'u*, made for the president of an association of Pacific Island women, expressed both regional pride and women's strength in organizing (Te Papa Museum 2016). In twenty-first-century Nunavut, Canada, Mother Hubbard-style parkas are associated with innovation and style rather than colonial domination (Sponagle 2014).

A conventional description of a Mother Hubbard dress in a United States museum collections database carefully describes the dress, but provides little indication of its significance: "Machine stitched. Skirt is gathered and attached over the bodice. . . . Self fabric belt. These kinds of utilitarian dresses or robes were made high-waisted, and relatively simple to put on . . . for work or when pregnant" (Five Colleges and Historic Deerfield Museum Consortium Collections Database 2016). The leap in meaning a museum would have to make between this type of basic catalog description and an interpretive approach that explores the agitation this object provoked, how the style traveled the world, or the dress's connections with women's work, sexuality, class, religion, or nationality is a long one. If the museum does not know who owned or created the dress, or does not have easy access to a specialist scholar, conventional interpretation is often limited to the information noted in collection records. However, the interpretive possibilities dramatically expand when the museum has access to resources to consider this dress both in a larger historical context and in terms of the public feelings associated with it.

This thought experiment reveals some ways in which public feelings and the contexts of those feelings could make collection items more active by bringing to the surface the sentiments associated with the object. Because public feelings are produced in specific times and places, it is possible to use interdisciplinary research and historical empathy to recover some aspects of public feelings. Such research is intended to provide enough context to generate interesting questions and provocative stories. How did it feel to wear a Mother Hubbard after having worn corsets under dresses? What caused some people to judge or monitor women who wore Mother Hubbards? How did women in Hawai'i make this dress part of their culture? Because this research is about establishing context, it provides specific details, but they are specific details that can help us understand many Mother Hubbards in many different collections, as opposed to the questions one asks of a single item (Who owned this dress? Who created that dress?). Therefore this research could be shared with any museum or individual interpreting Mother Hubbard dresses. An example of such research sharing is the theme studies for the National Historic Landmarks Program (National Park Service 2017), which provide historical contexts for interpreting the built environment. One can imagine a range of different types of commonly collected objects—spinning wheels, bottles of patent medication, radios, and butter churns—for which such contextual research could be made widely available to museums to strengthen their interpretive capacity.

Ivory Objects

Africans, Europeans, and Asians have valued ivory objects for millennia, but the material was an elite commodity. Elephant tusks, which are usually acquired by killing the animal or salvaging tusks from carcasses, were rare and expensive, and only the most skilled artisans could cut and carve ivory. The Industrial Revolution made ivory objects more affordable when factory owners in the Connecticut River Valley developed water-powered saws that efficiently cut ivory. Two Connecticut companies—Pratt, Read, & Company, of Deep River, and Comstock, Cheney, & Company, of Ivoryton—dominated America's ivory processing industry. The country's burgeoning middle classes bought ivory combs, toothpicks, letter openers, pistol grips, billiard balls, jewelry, fans, and ivory-handled brushes, knives, spoons, and forks. However, it was the piano that made ivory part of mainstream life in the United States. A skilled worker could create ivory veneers for forty-five keyboards from one tusk (Shayt 1993, 40). Families, houses of worship, and social organizations purchased pianos, spinets, and parlor organs, and with these acquisitions became part of global trade that fueled slavery and mass hunting of elephants in central and southern Africa.

Most of the ivory entering the United States in the nineteenth century was shipped from Indian Ocean port cities such as Mombasa and Zanzibar. These cities were controlled by coastal-based elites, who brokered trade between Africa's interior and the rest of the world. After hunters equipped with western-made firearms had killed many of the elephant herds near the Indian Ocean coast, caravans pushed toward the center of the continent, in the region that includes modern–day Malawi, Democratic Republic of Congo, Tanzania, Mozambique, and Zambia, and traded food, cloth, and other goods for humans and ivory. Enslaved men and women worked as porters, sexual partners, cooks, and laborers. When caravans arrived at coastal cities, new owners purchased many of the enslaved people and put them to work in households, farms, and clove plantations (Wright 1993). Others were sold into slave trading networks that included the Middle East, the countries bordering the Indian Ocean, and Brazil, until that country banned slavery in 1888 (La Rue 2012; Manning 1990).

The numbers associated with this trade were enormous. Ivory traders, including many from New England, purchased the tusks and shipped them to Europe or the United States. Ernst Moore, an American ivory broker who later denounced the trade, estimated that when he purchased ivory in the early 1900s, at least 20,000 tusks came into Zanzibar every year (1931, 214). In three decades, between 1870 and 1900, the firm Comstock, Cheney, & Company purchased about 200,000 tusks (Farrow et al. 2005, 209). By contrast, scholars have found calculating the number of people who were enslaved or died in the context of the ivory trade extremely difficult. Nineteenth-century Scottish missionary David Livingstone claimed that at least five African individuals—men, women, and children—were enslaved or died for each tusk that reached the coast. The stories of formerly enslaved people, recorded in the early twentieth century by missionaries and colonial officials, clearly reveal the violence and horror of the ivory trade (Wright 1993).

In the United States, many of the men who orchestrated the ivory trade were staunchly opposed to slavery in their country, but dissociated themselves from the bloodshed and slavery in Africa that fueled their wealth. However, companies promoted the connection between Africans, elephants, and pianos in their advertising literature. Bucolic images of elephants and Africans were intended to guarantee the quality of the company's ivory. One catalog cover, for example, juxtaposes an African man, who holds a spear with one hand and props up an enormous tusk with the other, with a White woman, resting near her piano in a comfortable Victorian parlor (Treasures of Connecticut 2016).

The men and women who worked in Connecticut's ivory processing industry were highly skilled. The workforce was predominantly White, including both native-born workers and European immigrants. The labor relations between employers and workers varied between paternalism and fractious strikes. By the end of World War I, the business of manufacturing pianos began a long, gradual decline, and with it, ivory cutting declined as well. Further, celluloid and other plastic veneers gradually replaced ivory on many ordinary keyboards. The last shipment of ivory entered Connecticut in the 1950s and Pratt, Read, & Company finally closed its piano parts business around thirty years later (Malcarne and Milkofsky 2016). The collapse of the ivory and piano industry was part of the nation's larger waves of deindustrialization.

This example of the museum objects related to the ivory trade provides an opportunity to explore the ways historical events can prompt new public feelings to surface in the present. In the late twentieth century, a loose coalition of local historians, journalists, museums, libraries, and historic preservationists began to explore the region's connections to the ivory trade. Through seminars, lectures, exhibitions, historic markers, books, and newspaper articles, communities in the Connecticut River Valley asked sophisticated, open-ended questions about historical responsibility, exploitation, slavery, and humans' relations with animals. How had today's residents profited from the earlier ivory trade? And how had this trade laid the groundwork for today's environmental crisis, in which African elephants are nearing extinction due to poaching? How could New England communities that vigorously opposed slavery and the slave trade in the United States have relied upon slavery in Africa? How can the exploitation of humans and animals be explored at the same time without trivializing either slavery or the ivory trade? Community members contended with their own complex public feelings which emerged as they learned about the ivory trade in the past and present: admiration of the region's ivory workers; anger at the continual loss of industrial work, which was evoked by the disappearance of the ivory cutting companies; shock, shame, and confusion when confronting a history of slavery about which they knew little; pleasure in the beauty of both elephants and the music produced by ivory-topped piano keys; anger at the continued killing of elephants for non-essential items; and guilt about the region's participation in the slavery and elephant hunting system (Daniels 2015; Joyce 2014).

The contemporary public feelings that emerge in the story of ivory are somewhat different than those explored in the example of the Mother Hubbard. The history associated with the ivory trade is emotionally charged but not well known and people encountering it for the first time may feel implicated or even ambushed by the facts. The contrast between the bloody ivory trade and an innocuous (billiard ball) or sublime (grand piano) museum object may be difficult to reconcile. Because the story involves slavery of African people, it is easy to imagine that discussions of the ivory trade may provoke responses analogous to museum-based explorations of the United States' history of enslavement, including guilt, deflection, denial, anger, and melancholy (Eichstedt and Small 2002; Rose 2005). Some of the public feelings that the ivory objects evoke would not be ends in themselves. Rather, as in the previous discussion of public feelings and mass incarceration, some public feelings, such as denial, may hinder empathy and action. Interpreters would need to be aware of these sentiments in order to facilitate greater understanding of the objects' history.

The research about the United States' involvement in the ivory trade demonstrates how this information can be used to provide greater context in interpretive situations beyond Connecticut. The organizations and individuals that initiated the exploration of Connecticut's connection to the ivory trade were largely motivated by curiosity about their region. But because the ivory processing industry was so centralized, this local history can also be used to understand many ivory objects in museum collections throughout the country. If an ivory object was produced in the United States during the nineteenth and early twentieth centuries, the raw ivory most likely came from African elephants and was processed in Connecticut. Thus this history and the associated public feelings apply equally to pianos in an Indiana history museum or ivory-handled cutlery in a Colorado house museum.

The charged public feelings around ivory objects could also raise larger questions about who produces an item. Typically, museums record the owner of an item or the individual or cultural group that created an object in the catalogue record or labels. It is intriguing to consider what possibilities would be opened if museums included among the producers of a piano or letter knife the Connecticut ivory cutters and people from East and Central Africa who were enslaved in the ivory trade. At the very least, the ivory trade's connections to today's pressing issues—slavery, exploitation of animals and natural resources, consumerism, and deindustrialization—when viewed through the lens of public feelings, provide opportunities for museums to engage in object-based discussions about these issues that introduce more nuanced, multi-faceted meanings.

As these thought experiments suggest, public feelings associated with museum objects can prompt creative, unsettling questions. An object may be associated with multiple, sometimes contradictory, public feelings. Considering public feeling requires a broader historical and social understanding of an object than is often provided or prioritized by museums, even those that follow best practices for collection management and interpretation. Like many of the ideas associated with making collections more active, collecting, documenting, and providing access to public feelings associated with objects pose a tension between continuing current museum practice, and making thoughtful changes that would make collections more engaged in contemporary life. When facing such choices, it is important that those working with objects understand the consequences of deciding to tell a "single story" about collection items, consequences that include reinforcing dominant narratives and diminishing the relevance of museums and their objects.

Museum professionals who are striving to make collections more active and relevant are searching for new stories; public feelings can be part of that process. Public feelings often focus on the everyday. Ann Cvetkovich writes that "richer accounts of the ordinary sought by Public Feelings projects are also new ways of providing the more systemic accounts of power that have been central to cultural studies" (2012, 11). Public feelings may provide a key to unlock alternative narratives of society and culture contained within the objects, many of them ordinary, which fill the shelves and cabinets of museum storage rooms.

References

Adichie, Chimamanda Ngozi. 2009. "TED Talk: The Danger of a Single Story." https://www.ted.com/talks/chimamanda_adichie_the_danger_of_a_single_story/transcript?language=en

Besley, Joanna. 2014. "Compassionate Museums?" *Museum Worlds: Advances in Research* 2: 133–169.

Biss, Eula. 2009. "Time and Distance Overcome." In *Notes from No-Man's Land*. St. Paul, MN: Graywolf Press: 3–11

Cummings, Maggie. 2013. "Looking Good: The Cultural Politics of Island Dress for Young Women in Vanuatu." *The Contemporary Pacific* 25(1): 33–65.

Cvetkovich, Ann. 2012. *Depression: A Public Feeling*. Durham, NC: Duke University Press.

Daniels, Marta. 2015. "Connecticut's Role in the Ivory Trade: Part II." *Quinnipiac Law Review* 33: 467–484.

Doss, Erika. 2010. *Memorial Mania: Public Feeling in America*. Chicago: University of Chicago Press.

Edwards, Elizabeth. 2010. "Photographs and History: Emotion and Materiality." In *Museum Materialities: Objects, Engagements, Interpretations*, edited by Sandra Dudley, 21–38. London: Routledge.

Eichstedt, Jennifer, and Stephen Small. 2002. *Representations of Slavery: Race and Ideology in Southern Plantation Museums*. Washington, DC: Smithsonian Institution Press.

The Empathetic Museum. 2016. Accessed November 28. http://empatheticmuseum.weebly.com/

Farrow, Anne, Joel Lang, and Jenifer Frank. 2005. *Complicity: How the North Promoted, Prolonged, and Profited from Slavery*. New York: Ballantine Books.

Five Colleges and Historic Deerfield Museum Consortium Collections Database. 2017. "Dress, 1890–1900, Accession Number HD F.135." Accessed March 29. http://museums.fivecolleges.edu/detail.php?museum=all&t=objects&type=ext&f=&s=&record=103&name_title=dress&earliest_year=1800&op-earliest_year=%3E%3D&latest_year=1949&op-latest_year=%3C%3D

Gray, Sally Helvenston. 2014. "Searching for Mother Hubbard: Function and Fashion in Nineteenth-Century Dress." *Winterthur Portfolio* 48: 29–74.

Jackson, Jessi Lee, and Erica R. Meiners. 2011. "Fear and Loathing: Public Feelings in Antiprison Work." *WSQ: Women's Studies Quarterly* 39: 270–290.

Joyce, Christopher. 2014. "Elephant Slaughter, African Slavery and America's Pianos." August 18. *Morning Edition*. http://www.npr.org/2014/08/18/338989248/elephant-slaughter-african-slavery-and-americas-pianos

La Rue, George M. 2012. "Indian Ocean and Middle Eastern Slave Trades." In Oxford Bibliographies in African Studies. Accessed November 18. http://www.oxfordbibliographies.com/view/document/obo-9780199846733/obo-9780199846733-0051.xml

Malcarne, Donald L., and Brenda Milkofsky. 2016. "Ivory Cutting: The Rise and Decline of a Connecticut Industry." Connecticut History.Org. Accessed November 15. http://connecticuthistory.org/ivory-cutting-the-rise-and-decline-of-a-connecticut-industry/

Manning, Patrick. 1990. *Slavery and African Life: Occidental, Oriental, and African Slave Trades*. Cambridge: Cambridge University Press.

Marks, Patricia. 2016. "Belva Lockwood and the Mother Hubbard Dress: Social, Moral, and Political Overtones in the Popular Press." *Journal of American Culture* 39: 298–312.

Moore, E. D. 1931. *Ivory: the Scourge of Africa*. New York: Harper & Brothers.

National Park Service. 2017. "National Historic Landmarks Program: Theme Studies" Accessed April 3. https://www.nps.gov/nhl/learn/themestudiesintro.htm

Passi, Peter. 2016. "Duluth's New Police Chief Acknowledges Great-Aunt's Role in 1920 Lynching." TwinCities.com. June 20. http://www.twincities.com/2016/06/18/duluth-police-chief-acknowledges-great-aunts-role-in-1920-lynching/

Rose, Julia. 2005. "Melancholia to Mourning: Commemorative Representations of Slave Dwellings at South Louisiana Historical Plantations." *Journal of Curriculum Theorizing* 21: 61–78.

Shayt, David H. 1993. "Elephant under Glass: The Piano Key Bleach House of Deep River, Connecticut." *Industrial Archaeology* 19: 37–59.

Smedley, Agnes. 1929. *Daughter of the Earth*. Mineola, NY: Dover Publications.

Sponagle, Jane. 2014. "Inuit Parkas Change with the Times." CBC News, December 30. http://www.cbc.ca/news/canada/north/inuit-parkas-change-with-the-times-1.2886115

Te Papa: Museum of New Zealand. 2003. "Woman's Dress and Hat. Registration Number FE001055/2." http://collections.tepapa.govt.nz/topic/1103

Te Papa: Museum of New Zealand. 2016. "Mu'umu'u: Dress. Registration Number FE012458/1." Accessed November 15. http://collections.tepapa.govt.nz/object/986352

Treasures of Connecticut Libraries. 2016. "Photograph of Catalogue Cover for Julius Pratt & Co. Goods, circa 1865." Accessed November 15. http://cslib.cdmhost.com/cdm/ref/collection/p128501coll0/id/1594

Winnipeg Art Gallery. 2002. "Life in Holman: Clothing and Shelter." http://www.virtualmuseum.ca/Exhibitions/Holman/english/life/clothing.php3

Wolcott, Victoria W. 2001. *Remaking Respectability: African American Women in Interwar Detroit*. Chapel Hill: University of North Carolina Press.

Wood, Elizabeth, and Kiersten F. Latham. 2014. *The Object of Experience: Transforming Visitor-Object Encounters in Museums*. Walnut Creek, CA: Left Coast Press.

Wright, Marcia. 1993. *Strategies of Slaves & Women: Life-Stories from East/Central Africa*. New York: Lilian Barber Press.

WHAT HAPPENS WHEN AUDIENCES "TALK" TO OBJECTS?

Gabriel Taylor

In 2013, Melbourne, Australia assigned email addresses to 70,000 trees in the city (City of Melbourne, 2016). The purpose was to allow people the ability to report any damage or vandalism to the trees. The actual outcome, however, was completely unplanned (Lafrance, 2015).

Emails were sent to the trees from passersby and from around the world. People saw the email program as a way to connect to the trees on a deeper, more emotional level. There were notes telling the trees about their beauty. There were notes describing how the trees helped passers-by get through their everyday lives. There were philosophical notes and funny notes and poignant notes. One email read:

> Dear Green Leaf Elm, I hope you like living at St Mary's. Most of the time I like it too. I have exams coming up and I should be busy studying. You do not have exams because you are a tree. I don't think there is much more to talk about as we don't have a lot in common, you being a tree and such. But I'm glad we're in this together.
>
> *(cited in Lafrance, 2015)*

What if we allowed audiences to talk to objects in our museums in the same way people in Melbourne talked to the trees? As museum professionals, we put our own interpretation onto an object and expect museum audiences to understand and appreciate that interpretation at face value. But in doing so, we can crowd out other equally valid and meaningful interpretations or ways of knowing an object. The beauty of the tree email system is that it makes room for many different ways of knowing and connecting with Melbourne's trees.

What would happen if we encouraged museum visitors to talk to objects in a museum's collection in the same manner people talked to objects in Melbourne?

We know that museum visitors' understanding of objects is shaped by their own experience, and thus not all visitors will engage with a single interpretation of an object. By interpreting objects without input from our audiences, we can create barriers to understanding instead of creating a meaningful connection. The beauty of the Melbourne tree email project is that it makes room for the many ways that people know, understand, and connect with the material world.

Allowing visitors to talk to objects with something as simple as an email or text makes it evident that some begin to see objects not only as "things" but as dynamic "beings" with a greater range of potential uses, possibilities, and stories. It empowers people to look for new layers of meaning in objects not only in museums, but in the world at large. Lastly, it allows museum professionals to learn as they begin to see new interpretations they might have previously overlooked. In this, we become better suited to assist our audience needs as we begin to understand and appreciate objects in different manners.

In taking this concept a step further, if a museum allowed visitors to "talk" to objects that evoke a certain emotional connection, what could happen if you enabled a visitor to talk to another visitor with a similar emotional connection to an object? Not only might they develop a deeper relationship with the object that was not previously visible, but the museum could also help facilitate an experience of social bridging between people who previously lacked a connection.

The success of the Melbourne project was a happy accident, but what if we did it on purpose? By encouraging visitors to talk to objects, a mutually beneficial phenomenon can occur. Visitors could gain a better understanding of the significance of a "thing" by first connecting it with their personal experience and values. Once this connection was established, it could open the door to other ways of understanding an artifact. At the same time, museum professionals would be exposed to other ways of knowing their collections, and thereby deepen their understanding of the potential emotional meaning and connecting points for artifacts. When we take a step back and relinquish some control, we can create a better learning environment not only for our visitors, but also for ourselves.

References

City of Melbourne. 2016. *Urban Virtual Forest.* http://melbourneurbanforestvisual.com.au/

Lafrance, Adrienne. 2015. "When You Give a Tree an Email Address." *The Atlantic,* July 10. http://www.theatlantic.com/technology/archive/2015/07/when-you-give-a-tree-an-email-address/398210/

4

HOARDING AND MUSEUM COLLECTIONS

Conceptual Similarities and Differences

Gail Steketee

Hoarding in History

Many of the questions posed by *Active Collections* consider whether current museum collections practices are healthy or sustainable. As a researcher and clinician who specializes in hoarding behavior, I was asked to shed light on what a person's relationship with his/her objects looks like in the extreme, when it reaches a state that is clearly unhealthy and unsustainable, such that it causes distress and impairment. A greater understanding of the extreme end of the saving-to-hoarding spectrum may help museum professionals clarify where their own practices lie on the continuum between healthy and unhealthy.

Collecting and saving objects is common to all cultures. Even nomadic groups carry with them objects that are useful, attractive, and meaningful within their culture. Early archeological evidence dating back 10,000 years indicates that hunter-gatherer groups hid supplies to secure them from other tribes and animals, much like scatter-hoarding (e.g., grey squirrels) and larder hoarding animals (e.g., hamsters, jays). Penzel (2014) reviews reports of early human hoarded items that included food, body ornaments such as amber beads, stone tools, and weapons, while more recent excavations (2,000 to 5,000 years ago) revealed hoards of religious objects (Egypt, China), coins, gold jewelry, and other forms of wealth (Britain, Greece, Rome). He also identifies miserly characters described in early Greek and Roman writings. Of particular relevance to library and history collections is the Egyptian library of Alexandria from 300 BC, which was thought to contain *all* of the world's knowledge in one very large collection of some 750,000 scrolls that unfortunately did not survive to present day.

Among writings about hoarding are Norse sagas such as *Beowulf*, which describes the hoarding of valuable objects that are guarded by both dragons and men. Many Biblical references eschew greed and the collecting of treasures, and even everyday items, for those who are urged to renounce worldly goods. In the *Divine Comedy*,

Dante Alighieri describes the fourth circle of hell in which Hoarders and Wasters challenge each other, illustrating opposing versions of the love of money and objects. Old misers who epitomize hoarding of valuable objects and money (e.g., Pantalone in the *Commedia dell'Arte*) appear in medieval and Renaissance writings. Closer to the current understanding of hoarding behavior is the character of Plyushkin in *Dead Souls* (Gogol 1842), who collects all kinds of objects including ones that are not clearly valuable; in contemporary Russia this character has come to represent someone with a serious hoarding problem. Likewise, Charles Dickens's characters of Scrooge (*A Christmas Carol*, 1843) and Krook (*Bleak House*, 1852) have become British and American models for miserly and hoarding behavior.

Hoarding as a Mental Health Problem

Interestingly, efforts to describe the phenomenon of hoarding as a mental health problem appear as early as 1809 with the term *bibliomania*, referring to extreme collecting of books—"the book disease." The notion that hoarding is both a human and animal instinct is evident in writings by psychologist William James, who implied that this was more than a character trait and might be considered a mental illness. Early in the twentieth century, conspicuous consumption and consumerism are described following the ready availability of goods in the wake of the industrial revolution. Freud proposed the "anal character" trait of parsimony, which could emerge as exaggerated greed and miserly behavior. Eventually, early psychological writings led to the inclusion of obsessive compulsive personality disorder (OCPD) in the American Psychiatric Association's 1968 diagnostic manual; it included the trait of being unable to discard "worn-out or worthless objects even when they have no sentimental value" (297).

It is not clear how closely our current understanding of hoarding behavior relates to the early descriptions of miserliness and greed. In any case, mental health researchers are generally agreed that collecting and saving behavior becomes problematic when carried to extremes, at which point it is called hoarding. Frost and Hartl described this problem in detail in (1996); they originated the term "compulsive hoarding" to distinguish it from normative behavior and further defined it as excessive acquisition and failure to discard items of uncertain value so that living spaces were cluttered and no longer usable, causing distress and/or impairment in functioning. Subsequent clarification of the definition based on research findings has led to the inclusion of hoarding disorder (HD) as a separate psychiatric diagnosis within the category of obsessive compulsive spectrum conditions (American Psychiatric Association 2013).

The hallmark features of HD (paraphrased from the DSM-5; see Table 4.1) are difficulty parting with possessions motivated by strong urges to save and keen distress about letting go of items. It is this attachment to objects that leads to the accumulation of too many things that are kept in a disorganized fashion, causing serious impairment in the ability to use the home and other aspects of everyday living such as social and work settings. Not surprisingly, hoarding often provokes considerable

TABLE 4.1 Summary of DSM-5 Criteria for Hoarding Disorder (APA, 2014)

A. Difficulty discarding or parting with possessions, even those that seem to others to lack value.
B. Failure to discard is motivated by strong urges to save items and distress about letting go of them.
C. Accumulation of a large number of possessions that clutter the home and interfere with ordinary use of rooms and furnishings. Sometimes, living areas are not cluttered because another person such as a family member or regulatory official intervenes.
D. Symptoms cause clinically significant distress and/or impairment in social, occupational, or other functioning, including maintaining a safe environment.
E. Hoarding cannot be attributed to another medical condition.
F. Hoarding is not better explained by the symptoms of another mental disorder, such as obsessive compulsive disorder, schizophrenia or dementia.
Specifiers:
Excessive acquisition
Insight (good or fair, poor, absent/delusional beliefs)

distress among those who live with or near the person who hoards. Interestingly, and perhaps especially problematic, is that the person with HD may have limited insight into how problematic and unreasonable their collecting and saving is.

As evident from the diagnostic criteria in Table 4.1, acquisition is not considered a defining diagnostic feature of HD. Nonetheless, evidence of current or past excessive acquiring is extremely common, occurring in about 90% of people who hoard according to recent internet surveys that assessed acquisition behaviors among people who self-identified with hoarding and from family members of such individuals (e.g., Frost et al. 2009; Frost et al. 2013). When researchers sampled people who met the diagnostic criteria for HD described above, again, a large majority (70–95%) met criteria for an acquisition-related disorder, including impulse control conditions such as compulsive buying and kleptomania (Frost et al. 2011; Mataix-Cols et al. 2013; Timpano et al. 2011). It is not surprising that excessive acquiring predicted distress and general, as well as social, impairment (Timpano et al. 2011).

Characteristics Associated with Hoarding

To provide some background on the general characteristics of people who hoard objects, it appears from epidemiological reports that 2–4% of the adult population report serious hoarding that would likely meet diagnostic criteria, and some estimates are above 5% (see review by Bratiotis and Steketee 2015). This means that most people know at least one, and often several, people with hoarding disorder. The average age of onset is in the early teenage years, with gradual worsening of the condition over time. Most participants in clinical research and treatment studies are middle aged, and it is apparent that hoarding is especially common among elderly adults. It is not clear whether hoarding is more common in women than men, although those participating in research or seeking help for their hoarding problem are mainly women.

Family studies indicate that hoarding is more common among first-degree relatives of people with HD compared to those without hoarding problems (Steketee et al. 2015). Hoarding is associated with lower rates of marriage and social activity, and some people report feeling more comfortable being around their objects than with people. About half of people diagnosed with HD also have serious problems with depression (~50%), and about a quarter suffer from social anxiety, generalized anxiety, and/or attention deficit disorder (Frost et al. 2009). Hoarding has also been associated with medical conditions like being overweight and chronic health problems such as cardio-pulmonary disease and diabetes. Among the hallmark symptoms of HD are indecisiveness that may partly stem from commonly found difficulty categorizing and sorting objects, as well as strong emotions that accompany efforts to avoid acquiring and to discard items. Certainly, these features contribute to the clutter, impairment, and distress.

TABLE 4.2 Belk's Definitions of Terms

Acquiring	To gain a feeling that the object "belongs to me" (although not necessarily legally), usually accomplished by purchase, but also by renting, stealing, gift giving, and creation (for example, by an artist or writer). A regularly used item (e.g., a particular chair) can seem "owned" by common agreement.
Possessing	Following acquisition, proprietary feelings arise, sometimes after specific efforts to personalize or render the object "mine." Use and habituation help to make objects "mine," as in the case of a common purchased item (e.g., a keychain, computer, car) that becomes "mine," having acquired a unique identity with regular use.
Owning	Individuals, groups, and the public (members of a city, state, or nation) can own objects and other property to which certain rights and responsibilities apply, including the use, sale, giving, or disposing of the property and protection from use by specified others. Ownership can include intellectual property (ideas, inventions, music, writings) and other "goods" (e.g., body organs) that may generate complicated legal disputes.
Collecting	The active, selective, and "passionate" acquiring and possessing of items that are not in ordinary use and are considered part of a "set" of non-identical objects. Collecting is distinguished from accumulation by the deliberate selection of specific items that constitute a cohesive set.
Curating	Curating refers to management of an existing collection after it has been assembled or bequeathed. Unless additional items are also being accrued for the collection, this work would not be considered collecting.
Accumulating	This generic term refers to simple acquisition of objects without a specified goal, though it could also refer to hoarding, for example, of 100 identical rolls of toilet paper that are not part of a "collection."

Of course, not everyone who accumulates large numbers of objects has a hoarding problem. Several writers have discussed attachment to objects from both normative and pathological perspectives. Belk (2001, 2014) defines and describes the meaning of terms like "acquiring, possessing, owning, collecting, curating, accumulating, and hoarding," noting that these activities can be carried out by institutions such as museums, curators acting on behalf of museums, and by individuals (Table 4.2).

Collecting vs Hoarding

To clarify the differences between hoarding behavior and collecting and curating as occurs in history and other museums, some discussion of the differences between *collecting* and *hoarding* is needed. A number of scholars have pointed to significant differences between acquiring in the context of hoarding and acquiring by "collectors" (Belk 2014; Nordsletten et al. 2013). The distinguishing features of these two phenomena are fairly clear as the summary in Table 4.3 suggests.

TABLE 4.3 Differences between Collecting and Hoarding

Feature	Collecting	Hoarding
Gender	More likely to be men	More likely to be women
Object attachment	Report attachment to and reluctance to discard objects	Report attachment to and reluctance to discard objects
Acquired objects	Narrower range of items within cohesive themes; a limited number of items are collected within categories	Lack of cohesive theme; many different types of objects; multiple purchases; duplicates are common
Acquisition process	Planned purchases of predetermined items; limited locations; mainly purchased or traded items	Acquisition often not planned or careful; locations not predetermined; both free and purchased items
Organization	Items are arranged, stored, and/or displayed; individual items can be easily located	Disorganized and cluttered; items are difficult to locate as similar objects are not necessarily kept together
Distress	Usually pleasurable; financial distress due to collecting is rare; less likely to report psychiatric problems	Considerable distress due to efforts to discard, inability to acquire and/or clutter; more likely to report psychiatric problems
Social Impairment	Low; more likely to have a partner; collecting is often a pleasurable social activity	Mild to severe; less likely to be partnered; relationship conflict and social withdrawal are common
Job Interference	Rare; little work impairment	Common; increases with hoarding severity

It is interesting that men appear more likely to be collectors, whereas women more often seek help for hoarding problems—although it is not clear that women actually suffer from hoarding disorder more often than men. Thus, this may not be a true gender difference, and might be affected by differences in societal perception of collecting and hoarding behavior in men and women (for example, are women's collections as highly valued as men's?). In recent decades, the majority of museum staff members in collections and education are women, and it may be of some interest to determine whether gender influences behavior toward museum collections.

As the table indicates, collecting is generally an enjoyable pastime that provides social engagement and often involves historical research to determine what items are valuable and active seeking of objects that expand the collection in ways that tend to increase its value. Such collections can be worth considerable money when the objects in question are of high quality and relatively rare. Examples of collections of historical interest include stamps, coins, writings and signatures of famous people, rare books, clothing and accessories, jewelry, games, photographs, memorabilia of all types, political buttons, war artifacts, clocks, types or periods of art, figurines, musical instruments, and cars. Such objects are the subject of TV shows such as *Antiques Roadshow* (PBS) or *American Pickers* (History Channel) rather than shows about hoarding such as *Hoarding: Buried Alive* (TLC) and *Hoarders* (A&E), which feature everyday objects that are often not well cared for.

What Lessons Can Museums Learn from Hoarding?

An interesting question raised by the above descriptions and definitions is whether there are lessons to be learned from understanding hoarding disorder and how it relates to the collections and curating needs of museums. This is especially true for history museums, which are faced with the accumulation of large amounts of information and goods that they may have difficulty displaying and storing. Among museum staff, curators have the most responsibility for decision-making about the collection, a strong investment in the outcome of their efforts and a responsibility to the board to account for their decisions. Does the very nature of museum collections predispose curators to decision-making difficulties with regard to whether to acquire new objects and/or to part with ones already in the collection? Curators may feel pressured to keep objects "for the sake of the collection." The next sections consider the similarities and differences of hoarding by individuals and the acquisition and management of collections by museums.

When Is Acquiring Excessive?

If not a required criteria for hoarding disorder, excessive acquiring remains a hallmark problem among those who hoard. Because almost everyone acquires items, an important question is when excessive acquisition becomes problematic. This same question faces museum curators and board members. The answer lies in the extent to which the acquiring behavior provokes distress and leads to impairment. In fact, distress and impairment are the critical defining features of nearly all mental health conditions—only when thoughts, feelings, and behaviors provoke personal distress and impair ordinary functioning can they be defined as problems. This may also be true for museum organizations. For individuals, impairment is evident when there is no space for newly acquired items that often live in bags near the door or in a storage area, there to remain for months and sometimes years because the purchaser has lost interest and the home is too full to be able to use them appropriately. Impairment is also evident when excessive buying leads to debt and diversion of the money needed for necessities to acquiring appealing objects the person seems unable to resist.

Dysfunction may be apparent when most waking hours are spent contemplating acquiring, seeking new objects, and/or becoming lost in fruitless attempts to organize objects so that other essential tasks are not done. The above disabilities refer to active acquiring that diverts space, money, and time away from other essential life needs. Acquisition can also be passive, as when others repeatedly give the person items because of their apparent interest in those types of objects ("Shirley loves handcrafts, so I'll just give these [unwanted, extra] craft items to her"). Likewise, junk mail, packaging of purchases, bags, and boxes might accumulate in the home with little active effort to acquire them. These latter passive forms of acquiring are problematic mainly because of difficulty in discarding (covered in the next section).

Museums may also be distressed and impaired by their collections—and despite professional guidelines, museum staff may feel powerless to solve the problem. From the museum perspective, professional guidelines put forward by the American Alliance for Museums (2012) distinguish between simple acquisition (acquiring of objects) and accessioning, which refers to the legal inclusion of objects in the collection. Accessions should be mission-driven to produce a strong and cohesive collection. This process should be done through written policy and may include an acquisitions committee that makes these decisions based on specific institutional policies. Thus, as for individuals, acquisitions are often active and planful, but items can also be passively accumulated (gifts, bequests) unless policies are in place to moderate this. Of course, policies must also be followed with reasonable accountability to accomplish their intended goal (see discussion about emotions, below).

Planned acquisitions presumably complement existing collections, filling in important gaps, for example in the historical period, geographic location, and/or historical figures that represent the museum's focus. These items might be acquired through purchase, trading with other museums, or gifting from donors upon solicitation. These acquisitions seem unlikely to cause impairment to the museum organization unless the money spent exceeds the budget allowed or the time required to acquire and process items does not allow for other critical duties. However, unplanned (passive) acquisitions may be a different story. These might arrive as gifts from organizations, including other museums, and individuals. The latter may have inherited objects they don't want to keep, and prefer to unload as a convenient tax write-off or perhaps to assuage guilt about parting with an ancestor's "collection." These same motivations may also characterize organizational donations. Interestingly, sometimes donor-gifted items may be inherited from a relative with a hoarding problem, arriving in a disorganized jumble and in less than pristine condition. Such gifts pose a special challenge for the museum curator and board members who must make difficult decisions about when to accept such gifts and when not.

When are museum acquisitions excessive? This question is, of course, a very different one from the ethical standards regarding responsible acquisitions such as those proposed for ancient artifacts by the Association of Art Museum Directors (see https://www.aamd.org/standards-and-practices). Applying the criteria of distress and impairment for individual hoarding to museums is not a perfect fit, but is an interesting exercise. Just as impairment in living space and daily functioning constitute criteria for hoarding disorder, acquiring and organizing that poses a burden on the museum staff, its budget, or the available space might be considered excessive. For example, when museum storage areas begin to resemble a hoarded home with disorganized piles cluttering the space so it is difficult to know where any given object is located and what it means, the museum might call a halt to further acquisitions until the existing objects are sorted, organized, and culled as fits the museum's needs. If staff have no time to devote to cataloging items, inventorying, and dealing with basic collections care and housing issues, that too seems a likely marker of the need to halt acquisitions. Of course, such costs in staff time, storage space, and expense must be weighed against the corresponding benefit to the museum's holdings and potential and planned displays for the public. Strategies for making such decisions are suggested in Chapter 10 in this volume.

Organizing

In addition to problems with excessive acquisition, museums also face difficulties typical of individuals with hoarding disorder in struggling to keep up with the need to organize and process all of the objects in their collection. Organizing is a definite challenge for many, if not most, people with HD due to what psychologists might call a cognitive processing problem whereby categorizing, organizing, and storing items does not come naturally. In some museums, objects are piled indiscriminately, and serious backlogs exist in basic cataloging, taking inventory, and physical management. This problem may stem from a large number of objects and lack of adequate staff to manage the load. Apart from an increase in funding for staff time and storage space, solutions to this problem will probably involve a deaccessioning plan while at the same time cataloging all retained items.

Attachment to Objects and Difficulty Discarding

People with hoarding disorder acquire and save objects for the very same reasons most people do—the objects have sentimental value, they are perceived as beautiful, and/or they seem useful. Sentimental value is highly idiosyncratic to the individual, often deriving from the person's heritage, history, and ultimately their identity. Examples of sentimental saving include a trinket acquired during travels, an heirloom passed down through the family, or a childhood toy with special meaning. Likewise, beauty and aesthetics lie in the eye of the beholder, leading people to save a wide range of items that may have little value to those who fail to perceive the attraction. Finally, many objects appear to be useful and in so doing are perceived to be opportunities offering attractive possibilities—like the broken chairs stashed in the basement that could be fixed and used or sold. ("I might need this someday" is a common statement such individuals make.)

For those with hoarding disorder, the emotional appeal, attraction, and potential utility of objects become exaggerated, making it very difficult to discard anything at all—even items that seem like trash to others. Even thinking about discarding can be highly distressing, provoking feelings of fear and anxiety, as well as grief and loss. These negative emotions subside when objects are retained: objects are therefore rarely released, provoking serious clutter problems with impairment that includes paths too narrow to navigate easily, important items lost in the piles, money spent replacing them, and damage to the home because repairs cannot be made. This list goes on, and gives a flavor that the impairment is a significant problem for the home dweller and others living in the home. Functional impairment leads to additional distress evident in feelings of being overwhelmed and unable to solve the problem, frustration, depression, and guilt.

Does something similar also happen for those charged with minding museum objects? Deaccessioning is the permanent removal of an object from a museum's collections (AAM 2012) and can be controversial, even as it represents good stewardship and refinement of the collection. As the American Association for State and Local History (AASLH 2012) specifies, "collections shall not be deaccessioned or disposed of in order to provide financial support for institutional operations, facilities maintenance or any reason other than preservation or acquisition of collections, as defined by institutional policy." Museums are urged to have policies in place that keep critics at bay, ensuring that the goal of removing items "is solely for the advancement of the museum's mission" and that not only the criteria for removal but also the decision-making process, disposal, and use of proceeds are clearly defined (AAM 2012).

Not surprisingly, the social and cultural expectations of museums are to protect and keep their objects. But as items are accumulated over many years, their sheer number can overwhelm a museum's capacity to display and store them, not to mention the ability to keep them organized in a useful fashion that allows decision making about what to rotate into display and/or keep for reference. Whether or not they are actively addressing it, many, if not most, museums face an ongoing need to deaccession items in their collection when their collections become too large or misaligned with their missions. With an ethical need to protect the public's trust and a legal requirement to follow proper procedures, deaccessioning is a complex challenge increasingly governed by regulations established by each museum. The guidelines retain a strong focus on the museum's mission in determining when to acquire new items and deaccession existing ones, but unfortunately, the guidelines also appear to encourage avoidance and inactivity in deaccessioning. Ignoring the problem is a natural response to the overwhelming task of deciding what to keep and what to remove from complex collections, and ultimately, it is the distress and impairment of overly large collections that forces the curator's and/or the board's hand.

An interesting question is whether the cognitive and behavioral processes are in the museum context also affected by emotions. For example, does deaccessioning provoke feelings of anxiety, guilt, and sadness among museum staff that make this process even harder than it might appear on the surface? This seems likely among museum staff who become anxious as they try to adhere to vague guidelines from professional groups, as well as complicated property laws that affect objects in the collection. Just as people who hoard often have family histories of hoarding and of other features (negative mood, indecisiveness, isolation) that render them more prone to acquiring and keeping items, does a museum's history and behavioral patterns figure into the difficulty in "letting go" of items? A further interesting question is whether some people who are drawn to museum curator roles are also inherently prone to excessive collecting.

Summary and Comment on Hoarding and Museum Collecting and Deaccessioning

Hoarding behavior has a long history that suggests it is inherent in human nature, undoubtedly derived from our mammalian ancestors. Currently defined, hoarding disorder focuses on difficulty parting with objects due to a strong urge to save them and distress at letting go, along with distress and/or impairment in functioning. Excessive acquisition is a typical accompaniment. Likewise, low insight about the problematic nature of the behaviors and the clutter is common and serious hoarding may be accompanied by social isolation, difficulty organizing objects and making decisions, and other psychiatric symptoms such as depression, anxiety, worry, and attention deficits. Hoarding is distinguished from collecting, and this distinction seems important in light of comparisons with museum activities of acquiring and deaccessioning.

According to the AAM, museums share the goal of collecting, preserving, exhibiting, and educating to promote scholarly understanding and public participation. A powerful ethical principle is that museum collections "represent the world's natural and cultural common wealth," indicating the very high value placed on museum objects as "resources for humankind" and the compelling goal to "preserve that inheritance for posterity" (see http://aam-us.org/resources/ethics-standards-and-best-practices/code-of-ethics). Interestingly, an analogy might be made to people with serious hoarding problems who may behave as if they are creating and protecting their own library or museum, a private trust as it were.

Museum collections are stewarded as if the public were their rightful owners and collections are permanent, requiring care, documentation, accessibility, and responsible disposal. Museums are expected to have mission-driven collections that are cared for, preserved, and documented, requiring considerable time and money. Deaccessioning is clearly expected, but also carefully restricted to respect preservation goals and conform to public trust responsibilities. While these constraints are obviously essential, they may encourage acquisition and retention of unwanted objects that cost time and money—removing from the collection items that are *not* mission-driven or *not* in adequate condition can be considerably more difficult than adding them.

BOX 4.1 Parallels between People Who Hoard and Museum Workers

- Both think every object is special and cannot pass up free objects, even if not needed.
- Both are unconcerned about having too many objects and share a goal of no loss of items.
- Objects induce positive emotions similar to the experience of an emotional high in both.
- Both experience emotional distress about object loss and experience impairment because of this. The distress stops museums from engaging in other activities because the overly large collection requires too much attention.
- Both believe "We might need it some day" and see opportunities in objects, sometimes with creative ideas about possible uses.
- Both assign meaning and identity to objects, varying only in individual identity vs museum mission.
- Both have stories about everything they own.
- Both underestimate their memory capacity. People who hoard fear they can't remember without seeing the triggering object. Museum staff believe their collections represent society's collective memory, fearing that without them, society would forget the history.
- Both believe objects stand in for people as if objects are permanent whereas people are not.
- Both people who hoard and museum staff seek to avoid waste, wanting to keep their objects out of the landfill.
- Both have limited awareness (insight) of their situation, believing their behavior is normal and reasonable, despite the distress and impairment.
- Both experience fear of making mistakes, of being irresponsible, and a desire for completeness of their accumulated items.
- Both avoid letting go of their stuff, making excuses to retain items.
- Both try to exert control over objects: "This stuff is mine, don't touch it!"

Box 4.1 summarizes some of the parallels between people with hoarding disorder and museum staff in settings with excessive collections. Chapter 10 provides some information about reducing clutter and controlling acquisition. Implications for museums facing some of the same problems are suggested in the context of the agenda to preserve and protect objects held in trust for the public.

References

Alighieri, Dante, and John Ciardi. 1970. *The Divine Comedy*. New York: W.W. Norton.

American Alliance for Museums. 2012. *Developing a Collections Management Policy*. http:// aam-us.org/docs/default-source/continuum/developing-a-cmp-final.pdf?sfvrsn=4

American Association for State and Local History. 2012. *Statement of Professional Standards and Ethics*. http://download.aaslh.org/AASLH-Website-Resources/AASLHProfessional StandardsandEthicsStatement.pdf

American Psychiatric Association. 1968. *Diagnostic and Statistical Manual of Mental Disorders*, 2nd edition. Washington, DC: APA.

———. 2013. *Diagnostic and Statistical Manual of Mental Disorders*, 5th edition. Washington, DC: APA.

Belk, Russell W. 2001. *Collecting in a Consumer Society*. London: Routledge.

———. 2014. "Ownership and Collecting." In *The Oxford Handbook of Hoarding and Acquiring*, edited by Randy O. Frost and Gail Steketee, 33–42. New York: Oxford University Press.

Bratiotis, Christiana, and Gail Steketee. 2015. "Hoarding Disorder: Models, Interventions, and Efficacy." *Focus: Journal of Lifelong Learning in Psychiatry* 13(2): 175–183.

Dickens, Charles. 1843. *A Christmas Carol*. London: Chapman & Hall. http://www.gutenberg. org/files/46/46-h/46-h.htm

———. 1852. *Bleak House*. Reprint, New York: The Penguin Group, 2003.

Frost, Randy O., and Tamara L. Hartl. 1996. "A Cognitive-Behavioral Model of Compulsive Hoarding." *Behavior Research and Therapy* 34(4): 341–350.

Frost, Randy O., Elizabeth Rosenfield, Gail Steketee, and David F. Tolin. 2013. "An Examination of Excessive Acquisition in Hoarding Disorder." *Journal of Obsessive-Compulsive and Related Disorders* 3(4), 338–345. doi: 10.1016/j.jocrd.2013.06.001

Frost, Randy O., Gail Steketee, and David F. Tolin. 2011. "Comorbidity in Hoarding Disorder." *Depression and Anxiety* 28(10): 876–884. doi: 10.1002/da.20861

Frost, Randy O., David F. Tolin, Gail Steketee, Kristin E. Fitch, and Alexandra Selbo-Bruns. 2009. "Excessive Acquisition in Hoarding." *Journal of Anxiety Disorder* 23(5): 632–639.

Gogol, Nikolai V. 1842. *Myórtvyjye dúshi*. Translated and annotated as *Dead Souls* by Richard Pevear and Larissa Volokhonsky, in *The Collected Tales*. New York: Random House, 1998. http://robobees.seas.harvard.edu/files/gov2126/files/gogol_dead_souls_1996.pdf

Mataix-Cols, David, Danielle Billotti, Lorena Fernández de la Cruz, and Ashley E. Nordsletten. 2013. "The London Field Trial for Hoarding Disorder." *Psychological Medicine* 43(4): 837–847. doi: 10.1017/S0033291712001560

Nordsletten, Ashley E., Lorena Fernández de la Cruz, Danielle Billotti, and David Mataix-Cols. 2013. "Finders Keepers: The Features Differentiating Hoarding Disorder from Normative Collecting." *Comprehensive Psychiatry* 29(3): 210–218. doi: 10.1016/j. comppsych.2012.07.063

Penzel, Fred. 2014. "Hoarding in History." In *The Oxford Handbook of Hoarding and Acquiring*, edited by Randy O. Frost and Gail Steketee, 6–16. New York: Oxford University Press.

Steketee, Gail, Andrea A. Kelley, Jeremy A. Wernick, Jordana Muroff, Randy O. Frost, and David F. Tolin. 2015. "Familial Patterns of Hoarding Symptoms." *Depression and Anxiety* 32(10): 728–736.

Timpano, Kiara R., Cornelia Exner, Heide Glaesner, Winifred Rief, Aparna Keshaviah, Elmar Brähler, and Sabine Wilhelm. 2011. "The Epidemiology of the Proposed DSM-5 Hoarding Disorder: Exploration of the Acquisition Specifier, Associated Features, and Distress." *Journal of Clinical Psychiatry* 72(6): 780–786.

5

THE *VITAL* MUSEUM COLLECTION

Elizabeth Wood

After the director's walkthrough of the museum's collection with staff, the recommendation was "just get rid of the brown stuff." At first this might sound like a demeaning assessment of the collection, but on further reflection, if you think about what that "brown stuff" was, it was quite literally dead wood. The director was referring to the non-descript, mostly drab, mostly wooden, ephemera. Much of this "brown stuff" was boring. It had no story, and frankly, had no place in the museum. It had no predictable future life in the museum and for all intents and purposes, was dead. Dead wood, in every sense of the phrase.

In a forest, dead wood is part of the overall ecosystem, but too much of it becomes dangerous. Nature's way of dealing with the overabundance of dead wood in a forest is through fire. The benefit of fire, at least in a natural sense, is that it brings rebirth and renewal to the forest. This natural cycle of life and death is important for the health of the forest and its long-term sustainability. It is not necessary to literally burn museums down to clear out the dead wood in preparation for rebirth, but we can begin to consider new strategies that reflect the potential that these cycles demonstrate.

When I think of making a collection more "active," I suggest that it be considered as something dynamic and alive. To think of a museum's collection as a living and contributing part of a museum's livelihood means changing some of our ideas about the fixed nature of collections materials. Instead of seeing the museum's collection as a constant or stable entity with the same things saved in perpetuity, we should look to ideas of variability and changeability, full of energy—as something vital.

Seeing the collection as a force of change to make a difference in the overall mission of the museum is critical; seeing it as a living system is a bit more radical— but the good news is there are other collections in fields as close as our library and archive cousins and as distant as the world's forests that have strategies that emphasize ongoing use and vitality of their collections. In each of these cases the changes are brought about by conscious decisions made by people, and we in museums have the power to bring about a new vitality in museum work. By drawing parallels between museum collections and the strategies used in fields like forest management and other "use based" collections like libraries, we might be able to overcome some of the greatest challenges that museum collections present.

Among the many tasks that we must overcome in creating the museum as an ecosystem is to see how words like "collect, preserve, and interpret" function as part of a living system. Those three little words permeate museum mission statements the world around. Yet, it is clear from the stories we hear, and the challenges we all know, that the "preserving" part of that mission is getting harder and harder. In fact, our own rules and expectations about what it means to take something into the collection, and what it takes to remove it are highly codified and fraught with ethical considerations. When we attempt to keep or preserve objects in perpetuity, we are effectively saying "we'll plant a seed and let it grow and grow (and grow), and keep it from harm, and keep it going well past our own lifetimes." We seem to have rationalized that our job is to keep everything forever. In reality, we just can't, and if we begin to shift our ideas about museums and to think of collections as part of an ecosystem, we might do a better job in maintaining collections that matter. Instead of suffering from "posterity anxiety," where every single object has potential, we should think about the collection being useful and enduring. This idea of enduring does not necessarily mean that the same things exist in the collection, but that the collection reflects a cycle of appropriate materials that expand meaning and purpose rather than limit it. That's where the forest and the library come in.

A Collections Forest?

One of the pioneer founders of the forestry movement, Gifford Pinchot (1905), suggested that the

> fundamental idea in forestry is that of perpetuation by wise use; that is, of making the forest yield the best service possible at the present in such a way that its usefulness in the future will not be diminished, but rather increased.

Pinchot's ideas suggest that a forest is not simply a one-time acquisition that we leave to its own devices, but that a forest is preserved by continually perpetuating it through constant decisions to add and remove material to promote vitality. Ideally our decisions about collections management mean that we are not limiting the use of the collection in the future by being shortsighted, or by never deaccessioning. Rather, by encouraging growth through choices of what to keep and what to dispose of, the forest is more likely to survive. Even in "old-growth" forests where human intervention is minimal, there is a constant cycle of growth and decay.

Forests, as living systems, are best maintained by thinking about concepts like "ecological succession," which encourages the continued growth and reproduction of the forest (Penn State University 2009). Within basic forestry concepts, there are four key requirements for a strong forest (Connell and Slayter 1977; Pinchot 1905), and each of these has a lovely connection to the idea of a museum collection. First that it is *protected* against fire, overgrazing, and theft. Second, that it have a strong and abundant *reproductive* process. It should always have young growth to keep it healthy. Next, there should be a regular *process for renewal*, by which trees come and go, and finally that there be *growing space* for every tree. It is easy to see the parallels between protecting the collection, and having room for each item. It is even reasonable to see the idea of forest renewal in a museum's process of acquisition and deaccessioning practices. But this idea of reproduction is the one that seems harder to grasp. How can a museum collection reproduce itself while at the same time providing sufficient space and protection? If our problem is trying to overcome too many objects in the collection, the notion of reproducing the collection seems like a bad choice.

Forest management practices were designed to maintain strong and healthy forests. To achieve the goals of overall long-term survival of the forest the field developed practices like harvesting, thinning, clearcutting, shelterwood, seed tree harvest, and prescribed burning. Thinking about these creatively within the museum collection could have a strong bearing on our work to carry out longstanding missions. Each of these forest management strategies has unique implications for thinking about the collection in terms of an ecosystem.

Transferring the ideas of forest management into museum collections requires that we first consider the museum collection made up of many parts—each of those parts relies on the health of the whole to make a difference. Taking on a whole and parts relationship (literally seeing the forest and the trees as the collection and its objects) provides new insights on how key practices of forestry could bring new life into museums. Imagine what it would be like to "harvest," "thin," and "clearcut" within a collection.

1. *Harvesting*: Harvesting is focused on improving the health of the forest. This is done by controlling the types of trees that grow in the area which might be better for attracting various types of wildlife, in creating sources of income for the landowners, or a harvest might make the land useable for recreation purposes. A regular harvest is meant to be done in proportion to what already exists in the forest. A museum's harvest or deaccessioning process should be similarly focused: the goal for deaccessioning should be about improving the role of the collection in relation to the museums goals or mission. While certain types of harvesting, like selling objects for income, is clearly against museum ethical guidelines, it is not out of the question to deaccession objects so that there is more space for new and different collections, or in using collections for broader purposes like educational programs, or transferring them to institutions where the objects are a better fit.

2. *Thinning*: In thinning the forest, the goal is to improve health and productivity by reducing the competition with other trees for resources. Water, sunlight, and soil are all finite resources in a forest and not all trees can or will be viable in an over-crowded forest. Imagine the implications of resources for objects

within the collection. Here too there are finite resources—maybe there are only so many light- or humidity-controlled spaces, maybe there's just not enough money in the budget to upgrade to a particular kind of shelving.

3. *Clearcutting*: While a clearcut is often viewed as an ugly blight, the purpose behind a controlled clearcutting is to convert unhealthy growth into something more sustainable. This is an effective process to create better generative behaviors for the forest. Generally the decision to conduct a clearcut is to provide greater access sunlight, which promotes better growth. Consider the possibility of clearcutting a part of the collection. Almost any museum will have some large, unwieldly set of objects that really drag down the collection—they take up too much space, they don't do much to support the overall collection, they waste time and resources to deal with. Opening up the storage space to give objects more space is not a bad thing. Getting rid of large swaths of the "unhealthy" or unnecessary objects in one process could do the collection so much good.

4. *Shelterwood Harvest*: Shelterwood is commonly known as the mature trees in a forest. When taken out over time, the space left behind promotes regeneration of surrounding trees. In a collection, there may be some venerable "oldies," but their time served has come and gone, and letting them go may free up considerable resources and space for more meaningful objects.

As with each step in the process to build a healthier forest, the goals for these activities are to support mutual growth and enhancement of the overall experience of the forest. When done properly, the forest continues to be productive year after year. On a practical level, in a museum collection, having a productive and active collection provides the museum with a greater connection to its audiences and ability to fulfill its mission.

Weeds in the Library

We all know that in nature weeds are opportunists and will fill the space if we let them. Moreover, weeds are often things in the wrong place—they may be useful somewhere, but not relevant or desired in a specific garden or plot of land. Gardeners must be vigilant in keeping weeds at bay so that they have an attractive, healthy, and purposeful garden.

Libraries, closest cousins to museums, have made considerable efforts to improve the management of their collections based on their missions. This is because "circulation" (another word evocative of a living system) is part of a library's main purpose in making its collection available to users. For a library, "items that sit on a shelf unnoticed or unused are a waste of space and budget" (Hibner and Kelly 2013, 13). To address this issue, the library field uses a process called "weeding" to continually review and renew the collections materials. Weeding is not a new idea to libraries as they have been discussing the idea of weeding out obsolete and out-of-date materials for over 100 years (Library Association 1900).

Key to the idea of weeding in the library is the recognition that the library is a living, growing organism based on the interaction of its collections and its patrons. There are two main orientations to weeding that are of use to building an active museum collection. Both assume ongoing and constant evaluation of use and need of the collection within the institution. The "CREW" model (Continuous Review, Evaluating, and Weeding) emphasizes ongoing assessment and consideration of materials and their use within the collection (Larson 2008). The process integrates both acquiring new material and "deselecting" of older materials that are no longer useful. The goal in the CREW model is to collect information on the strengths and weaknesses of the collection along with gaps and saturation points to further inform new acquisition. Clearly these ideas are not new to museum work and fall in line with deaccessioning practices. The difference is in how and what libraries do to make these decisions.

Libraries systematically monitor the use of their collections. As such, they have a well-developed system for tracking the most frequently used materials. Libraries can also follow various conventions regarding the use of materials based on age and copyright, and overall value to the mission and the audience. By keeping track of what is used and when it is used in the collection, libraries can make informed decisions that draw on their professional assessment and the needs of patrons. Given the consistent cataloging systems in libraries, the field has data on collections categories that further aid in the decision-making process of weeding. For example, the currency of information is primary for much of a library's collection in the social sciences, but maybe not so much for philosophy and literary classics. In those instances, librarians look to ensure that the collections do not reflect outdated ideas, but instead reflect quality scholarship.

Beyond the currency of information, which can be problematic from a museum perspective, one of the key considerations for weeding is the "MUSTIE" factor of books (Larson 2008). These principles of library weeding have great utility for museum collections as they further emphasize the relevance of the collection to the overall mission and purpose of the institution. MUSTIE stands for: *Misleading, Ugly, Superseded, Trivial, Irrelevant* to the community, and *Elsewhere*.

Misleading materials in a library collection refer to those that are factually inaccurate based on new innovations or discoveries in the field, changes in thoughts, and updated understanding of concepts. Within the museum, misleading collections items might be things that we don't have much information on and may not be verifiable, they might be poor quality, under-researched, or perhaps simply misleading with regard to what the museum is all about. There are countless stories in museums about objects donated by family members with rather auspicious histories that later turn out to be off by a few centuries. For example, a state historical society discovered a sword in its collection that the donor indicated had been carried by a relative in the Civil War, but further research indicated the sword was, in fact, made after World War I. This reiterates the importance of continued research and scholarship in collections and curatorial work.

In a library, the Ugly factor refers to lots of use—wear and tear, stains, dirt, and smells. These are things that most people don't want to touch! For museums there are certain reasons to consider the aesthetics of an object with regard to its overall appeal and potential to stimulate interest. In their research on "gateway objects," Francis et al. (2012) noted that attractiveness was an important feature of getting museum visitors to stop and look at an object. Ugly objects in the museum are probably least likely to be selected by internal teams and curators to put on display, too.

The Superseded item is one that has been eclipsed by a newer version. In the library world this refers to newer editions. In museum practice this can refer to duplicates or versions of the same object in different states of repair or quality or similar objects with various levels of provenance. Similarly, a Trivial item is one that reflects a fad or trend that is no longer popular. Museums documenting certain fads in history may be very appropriate, but there should still be a clear and focused reason or purpose for these in the collection.

Among the most valuable of the MUSTIE criteria is whether the material is Irrelevant to the community. In a library the materials on hand must reflect the needs and interests of the community to be used. For libraries, the "community" represents their regular users. In a museum, this concept is equally valuable. The more museums can begin to make room on their shelves for materials that represent members of the community they represent and their experiences, the more valuable the collection becomes to the community. But this means that museums must better know and be able to define their communities. Consider the implications that things like demographic change can mean for a community museum collection. For example, imagine a local history museum that serves a Latinx audience, but the museum's storage rooms are full of materials from elite, white settlers of the town. While the community changed around the museum, the museum still held on to the early material despite the fact that the collection limited the museum's ability to work with current audiences. Certainly not all the collection needs to go, but "there's little point in preserving collections if they don't actively support the mission. . . . **[C]ollections must either advance the mission or they must go**" (emphasis original, Active Collections Manifesto, this volume).

Lastly is the idea that a book might be found or obtained Elsewhere. Libraries have established a vast loan network that allows for sharing and reciprocal borrowing. This eliminates the need for every library to have every copy of every book. For museums, this presents a conundrum. Local museums should keep and maintain what is unique and important to their institutional missions; expecting museums to retain the same kinds of things everyone has in their collections is a problem. Building a more robust system for sharing collections, and knowing better who has what and where, might alleviate some of the biggest challenges of museum collections management.

The value of focusing on the library system of weeding is that it draws on the assumption that eliminating weeds leads to greater use of the materials that remain. Libraries have come to do the weeding process regularly as they continue to pay attention to use. The challenge for museums is finding ways to better track the use of materials. This might be better documentation or record keeping of what objects are regularly selected for display, requested for research, or considered for exhibition projects. It might entail taking time to look at categories of collections objects to track the appeal overall or developing new strategies for assessing their overall potential.

Sustainability

There is no doubt that one of the tensions between the forestry and weeding models and museum collections is about the role and purpose of museums in communities. As we have argued throughout the Active Collections Manifesto and in this book, museum collections can be powerful connectors to the human story, but only when used effectively.

If museums were to begin to work from a stance of the vital collection as part of the living, breathing, museum, we would be able to build more sustainable museums. In order to operate as an ecosystem, a museum must begin to recognize when it is time to let things go. To adopt a natural selection, so to speak, of artifacts does not mean we must discard everything. It means that we must make hard decisions about when it is time to let something go. Here too we can also learn from the lessons of forest management. In the twenty-first century, the potential for more catastrophic forest fires is a real threat. Human interaction, changes in policy, and overall population growth led to the buildup of too much fuel in the forests (Grant County Court 2012). Interestingly, we have the same problem in museums. The Heritage Health Index (2005) indicates that well over 630 million objects are in danger in American museum collections. Without a doubt there's a lot of "brown stuff" included in that number. It's time to really think about how we are managing our collections, or we too may face catastrophic results.

One way to consider managing collections is to think critically about how we in museums define use and what provides the highest potential for access. While such changes are complex, they are not impossible for a field that collects. In 2005 Greene and Meissner conducted a research project on the viability of processing and documentation of archives. Their survey of the issues and barriers related to archival practices is instructive for museum collections. The study "More Product, Less Process" (MPLP) emerged from the challenge of collections backlogs and the need for more realistic approaches. In particular, they sought

> to better appreciate the consequences of certain choices that archivists make every day, to understand and apply real administrative economies to the continuum of processing tasks, and to distinguish what we really need to do from what we only believe we need to do.
>
> *(209)*

Through their research, Greene and Meissner called for archivists to really think about the ultimate goal of their collections, and focus the profession's mindset around the use of collections and the accessibility of those collections for users. To this end, they created four criteria where archivists would emphasize a different set of standards that promoted vitality. The four criteria are: (1) to get users access to materials as quickly as possible; (2) to make adequate arrangement of materials to support user needs; (3) to take minimal steps for preservation; and (4) to describe the material adequate for promoting use. The simple shift in practice—the focus on the user rather than on preservation—revealed that the bottom line was that the profession needed to adopt new strategies and begin to implement them immediately. The end conclusion of the study was that focusing on getting materials more quickly in the hands of users was far more in line with the goals of the profession than simply requesting more time, space, or resources.

Conclusion

To create a vital museum is to have an active and meaningful collection that stimulates use and connection with visitors and that contributes to the museum as a living ecosystem. This requires courage to make decisions that are in the best interest of overall use and service. It means considering that the collection use is everyone's responsibility to define and to create. It means focusing efforts on the many different types of users and ways that the collection can stimulate user experiences and ultimately carry out the fundamental goals of a museum's mission.

We cannot let museum missions fall back to the old ideas of "collect and preserve" without a clear goal for the future. To have a sustainable future is to look for opportunities for reproduction and growth within the collection. We cannot just "protect" the collection like an under-managed forest. So instead of "collect, preserve, and interpret," museums should look to develop the museum and its collection as an ecosystem. As a living, and dynamic system that focuses on constant renewal, it can present a mission that looks toward maintaining a vital collection that reflects the needs of the community both present and future.

References

Connell, Joseph H., and Ralph O. Slatyer. 1977. "Mechanisms of Succession in Natural Communities and Their Role in Community Stability and Organization." *The American Naturalist* 111(982) (Nov.–Dec., 1977): 1119–1144.

Francis, David, Steve Slack, and Claire Edwards. 2012. "An Evaluation of Object-Centered Approaches to Interpretation at the British Museum." In *Museum Gallery Interpretation and Material Culture*, edited by Juliette Frisch, 153–164. London: Routledge.

Grant County Court. 2012. "Fire!" *Saving our Forests*. http://www.savingourforests.com/Fire.html

Greene, Mark and Dennis Meissner. 2005. "More Product, Less Process: Revamping Traditional Archival Processing." *The American Archivist* 68(2), 208–263.

Heritage Health Index. 2005. *A Public Trust at Risk: The Heritage Health Index Report of the State of America's Collections*. Washington, DC: Heritage Preservation.

Hibner, Holly and Mary Kelly. 2013. *Making a Collection Count: A Holistic Approach to Library Collection Management*, 2nd edition. Oxford: Chandos Publishing.

Larson, Jeanette. 2008. *CREW: A Weeding Manual for Modern Libraries*. Revised and updated. Austin, TX: Texas State Library and Archives.

Library Association. 1900. *Library Association Record 2*. London: Library Association. http://hdl.handle.net/2027/hvd.hnzh5q

Pennsylvania State University. 2009. *The Virtual Nature Trail at Kensington Station: Ecological Succession*. http://www.psu.edu/dept/nkbiology/naturetrail/succession.htm

Pinchot, Gifford. 1905. *A Primer of Forestry, Part II: Practical Forestry*. Washington: U.S. Department of Agriculture. http://www.foresthistory.org/ASPNET/Publications/primer_of_forestry/index2.htm

6

FOUR FORCEFUL PHRASES

An Archival Change Agent Muses on Museology

Mark A. Greene

I am an archivist. Not, as some have called me, an architect, artichoke, or anarchist. Just an archivist. Moreover, I am an archivist with years of direct experience working alongside and even supervising museum curators and registrars. I concur almost rabidly with the provocative assessments of the Active Collections Manifesto that people, not things, are the core concern of museums and archives. As best I can determine, provocation is exactly what's necessary to force the museum profession to, if you'll pardon the expression, get off its collective keister and run, not walk, into the twenty-first century of cultural heritage administration. I say this not from a belief that *my* profession has been, in general, any paragon of forward-thinking, but from the observation that archivists have awakened to certain realities, demands, and requirements for survival long before our museum colleagues have roused themselves—and with due modesty I take some credit for several of these changes in my profession.

Please permit me, then, to limn a handful of the most important changes embraced by archivists in the past quarter-century, and what similar changes in museum functions might look like.

I will start with a few attributes and definitions of archives. (Unlike museums and libraries, most individuals in North America have never heard of archives nor do they have the foggiest notion of what such a repository does; perhaps that is true of some of the readers of this book.) Most obviously, archives are, like museums and libraries, one of the cultural preservation and educational institutions in Western society.

Narrowly defined, archives are the records of the institution preserving them. Manuscripts repositories are collecting units, bringing in sets of material created outside the home preservation agency. "Special collections" often include not only archives, rare books, manuscripts, and audio-visual material (e.g., photos, films, videos, sound recordings) but also maps, artwork, and occasionally small aggregations of three-dimensional objects. More generally defined, as used in this essay, the terms archives, manuscripts repository, and special collections are interchangeable. Archives by definition are focused on primary sources (defined loosely, primary sources are those created at the time of an event occurring or created by an eye-witness even after the event), mostly textual and visual. Some, but not all, archives are parts of libraries. Public records archives are often part of the executive branch of local, state, or national government. Some large manuscripts or special collections repositories are either completely stand-alone—e.g., the Newberry Library in Chicago or the Huntington Library in San Marino, CA—or independent of the university library within a university or college.

Now, back to the main event. I take my general approach in this essay from one of the best addresses in the archival profession, presented by Maynard Brichford (head of the archives and special collections at the University of Illinois at Urbana-Champaign) in 1980 and titled "Seven Sinful Thoughts" (1980, 13–16). The essay, Brichford's benediction as President of the Society of American Archivists (SAA) is one of very few presidential addresses strong enough to not be instantly forgotten—archivists are elected president of SAA for many reasons, but their ability to deliver a memorable paper is not, evidently, one of them. The address has stood the test of time in part because it challenged then- (and even now-) accepted truths bluntly and with a touch of humor. Brichford organized his essay by stating each sinful thought as a short sentence and explicating it in a brief paragraph. I cannot think of a better approach to tackling my constructive critique, so herewith, my Four Forceful Phrases.

One: There Has Been a Longstanding Failure among Archives and Museums to Embrace Formal Collection Development Strategies (Greene 2015)

Collecting policies, as opposed to what might be labeled "micro-appraisal" (an assessment for acquisition of an individual item) has languished in my profession very demonstrably. Acquisition policies are necessary to ensure that collection development is planned, rational, tied to institutional needs and priorities, and realistic compared to repository resources rather than haphazard, knee-jerk, based on the interests or whims of individuals, and largely impractical. Yet a survey at the beginning of the twenty-first century (Sauer 2002) found that barely half of even the most elite special collections repositories in the US had formal collection development policies. A more recent survey of collecting policies on repository websites discovered only 38 policies out of 884 sites investigated.

This same survey also indicated reasons for abjuring collection development policies, including, tellingly: not enough time or staff; policy is not necessary; do not want to be limited by policy; no active collecting. The implication, supported by my interactions with hundreds of colleagues over the course of my career, is that planned, thoughtful, logical collecting—particularly that which best serves a repository's user base—is much less important than acquiring "stuff," lots and lots of stuff. For decades my profession has equated successful acquisition and appraisal with the *size* of the holdings on shelves, not with any sense of the *quality* of the holdings. As Canadian archivist Agnes Jonker notes,

The acquisition of private archives is diffuse, often led by serendipity and arbitrariness. In general, archivists find it hard to define an acquisition policy for the long term . . . Documenting society is an appealing idea, but how do we find out what is "significant," what is an "important event," or what is "representative," or a mirror of contemporary society? How do we decide that and based on what sources?

(Jonker 2009, 77)

The result is that "The evidence reveals . . . incredible gaps in the documentation of even traditional concerns" and further "showed that many archivists waste time and space preserving random bits and pieces, as well as large accessions, of the most dubious value" (Ham 1975, 6). The appearance to an outsider, critics have noted, may be less that of a professional selecting what matters and more of a community attic.

Even when collecting policies are present, they may not be functional: the 2001 survey discovered that repositories with written collecting policies were far more likely than those with informal policies to accession a collection because of a fear the collection might otherwise be destroyed, even though the material did not fit within the policy (Sauer 2002). As another critic has complained, "[O]ur instinct is still to see ourselves [as] the last line of defence between preservation and oblivion. This causes us to make utterly ludicrous decisions regarding acquisition by [assuming] . . . the virtue of maintaining culture: if I don't save it, who will?" (Ericson 1991–1992, 69). This question is one of the biggest obstacles to Active Collections. While it may at times be true that rejecting a potential acquisition will lead to its destruction (or retention in private hands), it is also at times true that the acquisition either can and should find a home at another repository or that it deserves destruction or inaccessibility in the family's closet. As Tim Ericson forcefully reminds us,

In determining whether or not to acquire a set of records, archivists should first decide whether or not the records themselves contain evidential or informational content. But having done so we must then pause to ask, "So what?" The final decision regarding whether to acquire an individual [collection or item] must be made with an eye on the larger universe that is defined by broader acquisition development policies. Stated another way, the principles of appraisal help us to answer the question, "*Why* am I saving this?"—while acquisition policies force us to answer the equally important question, "Why am *I* saving this?"

(Ericson, 1991–1992, 68)

Both archives and museums routinely, and I would say blithely, refer to documenting society or to seeking to "hold up a mirror for mankind" (Ham 1975, 13). Repositories do not see rational collections development as a major concern or even at the core of what they do. This shows that their major focus remains on their own internal preoccupations and not those of the end user.

Good collecting policies, when followed, accomplish even more than improving the selection and appraisal of collections for a repository. A formal policy demonstrates a clear degree of professionalism when the repository's parent administration, as it always should, endorses it; it also helps ensure that the administrators understand what the repository is doing and why. Thus they are more likely to (a) back up the staff if a donor complains and (b) not sabotage the policy by making unilateral decisions to accept collections. It permits the repository to accurately allocate resources to reasonable goals. Explaining negative acquisition decisions to donors is much easier when the decisions are based on formal policy. A collecting policy permits reassessment as time passes—thus a policy also permits reappraisal.

So far I have analyzed and criticized my own profession for neglecting collection strategies, but I ask you to substitute "museum" for "repository" and see if you don't agree that the shoe fits the other foot equally well. Consider the implications of collecting policies for the Active Collections Manifesto's calls to: "discuss collections at the board level" (collection strategies should be vetted by your board); "not accept artifacts you do not need" (how do you know if you need them if you haven't defined collecting goals and priorities?); and stop acquiring items just because nobody else will (see Active Collections Manifesto, this volume).

Two: Once a Repository Has Defined What It's Collecting and Why It's Collecting It, Such an Institution Should Be Willing to Jettison Everything That Does Not Fit the Collecting Policy (Greene 2010a)

It is long past time for reappraisal to be "a word never uttered aloud" (Shelstad 1998, 144). Suffice it to say here that I have never found any of the objections to reappraisal and deaccessioning had the least merit, so long as the repository did four things: (1) developed a written deaccessioning policy, approved by the highest institutional official possible; (2) approached reappraisal and deaccessioning as normal collection management steps, and not as frantic emergency measures once shelf space is gone; (3) already had in place a formal collecting policy; and (4) conducted its project transparently rather than trying to keep it a secret.

These pieces were in place at both the institutions where I conceived, directed, and helped carry out major reappraisal and deaccessioning projects. At the Minnesota Historical Society (MHS), I reappraised the contents of its six post-World War II congressional collections, based on a newly developed set of appraisal guidelines, and reduced their size an average of 64% totaling 1,000 cubic feet. In several instances, because of the terms of the deeds of gift, we had to get permission from the donors—from sitting U.S. Representatives, individuals whom archival common wisdom maintained had egos so massive that they believed every scrap of their papers was of major historical importance. But our contact included an explanation of the "what and why" of our new guidelines, as well as an argument that by "focusing" their collections researchers would be able more easily to home in on the material that reflected the congressperson's most important accomplishments. We not only received permission to reappraise and jettison hundreds of boxes from every individual contacted, we did not even elicit any questions, much less concerns (Daniels-Howell 1998; Greene 1994).

At the University of Wyoming's American Heritage Center (AHC), all of these measures were in place as well. Its reappraisal and deaccessioning policy and process was part of its collection management policy; the Center undertook its vast reappraisal project under no duress of shelving space; its new collecting policy identified what the repository *did* want, therefore it also defined what the AHC *didn't* want; and the repository publicized its reappraisal and deaccessioning project not only on campus, but through its newsletter, delivered to more than 4,000 of the Center's financial supporters, collection donors, and other interested parties. This mass publicity about what archivists in the US generally consider a politically suicidal, if not ethically suspect, activity, engendered a mere half dozen polite, curious, inquiries.

Following these steps, the Center completed what it believed to be the largest reappraisal and deaccessioning project of private archives in U.S. history (Greene 2002; Greene 2006; Jackson and Thompson 2010). As part of a grant to catalog our unprocessed collections, the Center surveyed 2,292 collections, of which 700 were subsequently cataloged and 1,592 identified for possible deaccessioning. During the second half of the grant, 414 collections on the potential deaccessioning list—all those larger than 10 cubic feet—were reappraised, of which 77% were deaccessioned. Those not deaccessioned were either cataloged, transferred to the university's library, or deferred for additional investigation. The deaccessioned collections totaled 13,300 ft. Fifty-five percent of deaccessioned collections were transferred to other repositories, 5% are still looking for an appropriate repository, 8% were returned to donors, and 9% were destroyed. The Center transferred collections to 164 repositories in 42 states and six countries, including to Bristol University and the British Film Institute. Less than a year after the end of the grant-funded deaccessioning we surveyed 100 repositories to which we had transferred collections. While 50% of these collections were, though after a relatively brief period, sitting in a processing queue, a remarkable 38% had already been processed and were being used by researchers.

Did AHC donors revolt? Hardly. Of the 320 collections deaccessioned, three donors or their descendants expressed displeasure. Of these, two were mollified once I explained in detail the policy basis of our decision, and particularly that we had not targeted their particular collection. The one donor who remained upset represented a minute percentage of the total. On the other hand, five of these donors actually went so far as to thank the archives for how it handled the whole matter, and three of those actually sent checks in appreciation!

Moreover, my university's provost was delighted with our new approach for two reasons. One was that the deaccessioning was a palpable exercise in demonstrating our new commitment to rational, policy-based holdings, rather than the indefensible hodge-podge created by the earlier director. Second was that the Center was clearly committed to making the most rational, efficient use of our resources—not only of its shelving space but also of its processing personnel; every collection deaccessioned represented one less collection that had to be arranged and described.

It is no small irony that the Society of American Archivists' recently adopted Guidelines for Reappraisal and Deaccessioning, which "Establishes a step-by-step approach to reappraisal and deaccessioning in archival repositories and outlines general steps, problems, and solutions yielding responsible and ethical reappraisal and deaccessioning decisions" (SAA 2012), was based almost wholly on that developed by the AHC and that the Center's version was based very greatly on that developed by the American Association of Museums in the 1990s. Hence, archivists have, at least in concept, finally accepted reappraisal and deaccessioning as a standard collection management tool; it would be immensely ironic if, at the same time, museums turned their back on these processes—particularly if that rejection was based on improper application of the standards in the first place (see Anderson 2015).

Three: Refusal to Accept the Problem of or Devise Solutions for Enormous Cataloging Backlogs, a Problem for All Three Cultural Heritage Professions (Greene 2008, 2013)

Of course I would love to do more—more description, more preservation—but I have come to realize that the resources necessary for that level of work will never come. If we continue to approach our backlogs with the idea that we just have to hold on until that wonderful day when the money people finally realize our value and hand over whatever we need, then we are doing our researchers, our staff, and those collections languishing in "unprocessed" limbo a severe disservice (Foster 2006, 5).

If I had a mantra, as the director of a large research repository at a land grant university, it was "Let's try to give our users what they want." My experiences in all four of the institutions in which I worked ignited in me an almost frantic zeal to address the problem that in 2003 came to be known as "Hidden Collections" (Jones 2003) but which I knew much more familiarly as "backlogs." (More wryly, the Library of Congress at the time referred to its uncataloged and unprocessed collections as their "processing reserve.") In archives and manuscripts repositories across the nation, the mean portion of collections unprocessed was then roughly 33% (Greene and Meissner 2005, 210).

All of my institutions had immense backlogs. I first became truly alarmed at the backlogs in Minnesota because I was the acquisitions curator, and it made my donor relations difficult to have to tell a prospective contributor of a collection that the material would not be processed for many, many years. At the historical society it was equally stressful to have to explain to a donor's heirs why after a decade their father's papers were still in the original boxes with no catalog record or finding aid; much more distasteful was explaining the delay when the donor or his/her heirs complained not to me but to the director or president of my institution. So those hidden collections were making my life occasionally miserable.

While 70% of repositories admitted their own backlog was a serious problem, almost 80% of archives continued annually to acquire more collection material than they could process in that time (Greene and Meissner 2005, 211). It seemed to me then that the good ship archives was taking on water, and its crew was busily drilling more holes. Does this sound at all familiar?

I once encountered a situation at The Henry Ford where the registrar was also faced with cataloging thousands of campaign buttons and as traditional practice dictated was approaching the task one button at a time. I tried to convince her that it was not only possible, but essential in the face of the museum's enormous cataloging backlog, that the buttons be cataloged in aggregate—not all buttons in one catalog record, of course, but for example, all 1972 election buttons in one record, and so on, or failing that all of George McGovern's buttons in one record. It would then be a simple matter to locate, for instance, buttons featuring McGovern and his running mate. I could not budge her.

After I ascended to the directorship of the AHC, and after considerable research supported by the National Historical Publications and Records Commission, in 2005 a colleague of mine from the MHS and I published an article that unwittingly created what some have called a "revolution." What has become known as MPLP or Greene-Meissner or "minimal processing" argued that archivists must increase the quantity of archival material accessible to users by increasing the speed of cataloging at the expense of traditional notions of quality: in archival terms abjuring item-level precautionary preservation steps such as photocopying news clippings and removing all metal fasteners; also, and most importantly, first cataloging all collections at the highest aggregate level possible and only then returning to some of the most significant collections to catalog at more granular levels (Greene and Meissner 2005; Greene 2010b; Meissner and Greene 2010).

When I arrived at the AHC its holdings were close to 90,000 cubic feet and approximately three quarters of our collections were unprocessed and uncataloged; we did permit access to unprocessed collections, if a researcher could find them without any information online. Within five years of establishing our minimal processing approach, the Center had no more hidden collections. Instead of traditionally arranging and describing some 60,000 cubic feet of manuscripts and archives, a task that would have taken decades, the AHC first created collection-level Machine Readable Catalog (MARC) catalog records, published in our Online Public Access Catalog (OPAC) and in the World Catalog (WorldCat), for every one of our collections. Then it converted all the catalog records to Encoded Archival Description (EAD), so they would be accessible through a standard web search.

There is direct evidence that our many and disparate users prefer "more" over "better" at a ratio of about two-to-one: When 600 mixed survey respondents, including scholars from many disciplines, were asked to "rank a list of archival activities in order of importance to them, a large margin ranked first 'Putting more resources into creating basic descriptions for all collections, even though some of those collections may never have more detailed inventories written for them'" (Greene 2010b, 184). As one assessment of our approach summarized,

> Greene and Meissner's study . . . served to confirm what many have long known or suspected: archival processing tends to be so expensive and time-consuming that it prohibits archivists from processing materials and making them available to users . . . Instead, [Greene and Meissner] suggest

that archivists must evaluate how they conduct processing, and to learn to better differentiate between necessary practices and the practices that archivists have convinced themselves are necessary.

(Coyner 2009, 4)

It does not surprise me, then, to find, in Robert Janes's essay in this volume, a very similar assessment of museums: "The reality is that individual museums are simply too bound by the inertia and expense of curatorial and institutional requirements," he avers. "The complex nature of the curatorial process, including the procedures, the time, the energy, and the resources required, creates an internal inertia which few, if any, museums can overcome" (Janes, this volume). Hear, hear!

Four: The Compulsion to Obsess about Means Rather Than Ends, Process Rather Than Mission, and Collection Material Rather Than Use or Users (Greene 2009a)

I titled one of my professional presentations "Existential Archives: Looking to the Value Propositions of Archives and Special Collections." That paper began with this quotation: "'The worst thing that could possibly happen to anybody . . . would be to not be used by anyone for anything'" (Vonnegut 1974, 18). In this quote from a character in *Sirens of Titan*, Kurt Vonnegut sums up my assessment of the value of special collections—to be used, and used often, well, and even passionately. I will go so far as to say that everything—*everything*—a special collections archivist, curator, or librarian does should be done with this in mind. *Use*, in its most general sense, is, to quote a groundbreaking archival author of the mid-twentieth century, "the end of all archival effort" (Schellenberg 1956, 224).

Rare book librarians, special collections curators, and archivists have for too long treated their collections as ends in themselves; the tidy books or boxes on shelves as the point of their work, taking pride in the growing numbers of things rather than a growing number of users. This resulted, to be sure, in the acquisition of some fabulous historical documentation, but too often such acquisition was driven more by the glory of bagging a high-profile donor or by an intuition than by concern for building collections that would best engender use. Many museums have lulled themselves into believing that they are documenting particular subjects well simply because they have many related objects to show for their efforts.

Every museum of any size possesses . . . great quantities, of material which it cannot hope to display and . . . duplicates of items already on exhibition. [One museum] has, for example, more than two hundred eighteenth-century pottery milk-jugs, in the form of a cow. They ranged side by side on a shelf . . . like some huge herd on a farm. This is investment banking, not museology.

(Hudson as cited in Ericson 1991–1992, 70)

For me, I believe Brichford was correct twenty years ago when he suggested that "*use* of the archives and the growth of its reputation" was "the surest proof of sound records appraisal" (Brichford 1977, 1, emphasis added).

I asked our processing manager at AHC to ramp up the changes to processing and cataloging over three years, 2002–2005. The first year her department eliminated removal of metal fasteners and organizing material within folders, and achieved a doubling of cubic feet processed. The next year the Center eliminated most re-foldering, re-boxing from record center cartons to flip-top boxes, photocopying newspaper clippings, and sleeving torn items, and achieved another doubling of cubic feet processed. The third year, beginning to use NHPRC grant funds, the AHC shifted most processor time to cataloging unprocessed collections, with the goal of providing basic intellectual access to all of the collections that the collection analysis (being carried out in tandem with the processing work) indicated would be retained. In two years (2005–2007) the repository accomplished that feat, making all of its collections visible to researchers; in subsequent years the goal was to return to processing in greater detail the now-cataloged collections. Simultaneously, to help prevent future uncataloged, unprocessed backlogs, the Accessioning department overhauled accessioning procedures to include creation of skeletal MARC records and box-level description.

Why did we do all this? To expand, promote, and sustain use, use by our entire spectrum of researchers, from grades 4–6 to senior scholars and certain professionals (e.g., attorneys, reporters, land managers). The 2008 "Report of the WorldCat Local Special Collections and Archives Task Force" states flatly:

> The rare books, manuscripts, archives, and other special collections materials in research libraries have become widely recognized as the hallmarks of distinction of individual academic libraries, as their general collections become increasing homogenized through the acquisition of licensed content and digitized books.
>
> *(Online Computer Library Center 2008, 1)*

Hence use of those collections is becoming more and more significant to libraries.

However, there is abundant evidence that the broader special collections community continues to wrestle with the degree to which it should expand use. Again, rare book librarians, special collections curators, and archivists have for too long treated their collections as ends in themselves—the tidy books or boxes on shelves as the point of their work—and regarded with protection at best and displeasure at worst the requests by even "qualified scholars" to possibly sully or disorganize their precious "things." Collecting, not even cataloging, was their end. There are still too many archives and special collections that hold this worldview. I know this not only from talking to researchers, but also from the fact that when archivists from the AHC gave presentations at the Society of American Archivists annual meetings on our active outreach to grades 6–12 and undergraduates, they received comments indicating quite clearly that some of our colleagues were thoroughly surprised, while a few thought we were quite mad. A 2006 survey of elite Association of Research Libraries special collections discovered that a full third declined to host any pre-college classes (Visser 2006, 315).

We know that our institutions and society cannot and should not support with resources the simple instinct to preserve. We provide a professional assessment of what should be preserved, and why. Otherwise, we wind up arguing that we need more space, and more staff, to store more and more stuff that nobody actually uses. Society, Gerry Ham wrote in the 1980s, "must regard such broadness of spirit as profligacy, if not outright idiocy." Ultimately, archives and archivists are foremost about people and not things—we serve our users first, not our collections (as cited in Greene 2009, 30, 32). To partly paraphrase Janes (this volume),

> We need to set aside our professional servitude to collections for collections' sake and think more deeply about their use in creating personal meaning and collective wisdom . . . Every museum, irrespective of size and subject, can make this connection between the collections and knowledge they hold, and the issues and challenges that confront society now.

"We Are Keepers for a Purpose"

To increase use requires, among other things, to analyze what's on the archive's shelves in order then to accurately develop a collection development policy that best reflects the repository's mission and resources, and the needs of its clientele; to actualize that collecting policy by actively soliciting new material, whether to fill gaps or to further build strengths; and to make the ultimate commitment to the collection development policy by identifying reappraisal and deaccessioning projects. This last activity will not only increase use of your holdings, by among other things giving over shelf space to collections more relevant to your own users, it will also increase use of some deaccessioned collections by placing them in institutions where they will be better understood, more quickly processed, and more visible to likely researchers.

George Bernard Shaw is purported to have said: "This is the true joy of life, the being used up for a purpose recognized by yourself as a mighty one" (Shaw, 1903). I believe firmly that the mission of archives and museums is to have their collections be used, though whether for mighty purposes or trivial ones is actually not for us to choose. Everything an institution does should be supporting the end goal of increasing the use of its holdings—use, by the way, that includes not solely researchers in the reading room or viewing digitized collection material on our websites, but also viewing our in-house and traveling exhibits, employing facsimile packets in the classroom, listening to or reading scholars who have used our holdings, watching documentaries that highlight some of our photographs and objects, and the like. Use should be the end of all our efforts; if not, just what are we collecting all this stuff for? To end about where I began, with Brichford's "Seven Sinful Thoughts," let me put forward for my museum colleagues one of his complete propositions:

A fourth thought is to "let them rot"; i.e., documents that need the conservator's attention, if they are to be preserved for posterity, may not be worth the cost of conservation. Item conservation without appraisal of the value of the documents is an exercise in futility. The millions of cubic feet of records in archival custody cannot be preserved forever. Heretical though it may be, I suggest that we have wasted a lot of money placing acid-laden documents in acid-neutral folders and boxes, in deacidifying surfaces and in purchasing expensive physical facilities at the expense of public service . . . *We are keepers for a purpose and that purpose is not "keeping," but using.*

(*Brichford, 1980, 14, emphasis added*)

I enthusiastically commend the Active Collections Manifesto for entreating, in unmistakable language, my museum colleagues to embrace the commitment to use—active, broad, eager use—that my archival peers have gradually accepted as their reason for being.

References

American Heritage Center, University of Wyoming. 2008. *Collection Management Policy.* http://ahc.uwyo.edu/documents/about/administration/coll%20mgt%20policy%20 3d%20rev.pdf.

Anderson, David. 2015. "In Defence of Inviolability: The Value of Museum Collections." *ICOM News* 1: 14–15

Brichford, Maynard J. 1977. *Archives and Manuscripts: Appraisal and Accessioning.* Chicago: Society of American Archivists.

Brichford, Maynard. 1980. "Seven Sinful Thoughts." *The American Archivist* 43(1): 13–16.

Coyner, Libby. 2009. *Economy of Effort and the "Acceptable Minimum": Exploring the "More Product, Less Process" Approach to Archival Processing.* Thesis for MAS at School of Library and Information Science at University of British Columbia.

Daniels-Howell, Todd. 1998. "Reappraisal of Congressional Papers at the Minnesota Historical Society: A Case Study." *Archival Issues* 23(1): 35–40.

Ericson, Timothy L. 1991. "At the 'Rim of Creative Dissatisfaction': Archivists and Acquisition Development." *Archivaria* 33: 66–77.

Foster, Anne L. 2006. "Point-Counterpoint: In Favor of Minimum Standards Processing." *Easy Access* 32: 5–7.

Greene, Mark. 1994. "Appraisal of Congressional Papers at the Minnesota Historical Society: A Case Study." *Archival Issues* 19: 31–44.

———. 2002. "What WERE We Thinking? Embracing Reappraisal and Deaccessioning as a Collection Management Tool." *Provenance* 20: 33–49.

———. 2006. "I've Deaccessioned and Live to Tell About It: Confessions of an Unrepentant Reappraiser." *Archival Issues* 30: 7–22.

———. 2008. "Trying to Lead from Good to Great and Some Reflections on Leadership at All Levels." In *Leading and Managing Archives and Records Programs: Strategies for Success,* edited by Bruce Dearstyne, 137–162. New York: Neal Schumann.

———. 2009a. "Existential Archives: Looking to the Value Propositions of Archives and Special Collections." Unpublished paper presented at the joint Association of Research Libraries/Coalition for Networked Information Forum, "An Age of Discovery: Distinctive Collections in the Digital Age."

————. 2009b. "The Power of Archives: Archivists' Values and Value in the Post-Modern Age." *The American Archivist* 72: 17–41.

————. 2010a. "'If You Cannot Get Rid of the Family Skeleton, You May As Well Make It Dance': How One Repository Tangoed Successfully with Some Controversial Collection Management Activities," Research Library Group Partnership European Meeting, "Moving the Past into the Future: Special Collections in a Digital Age," Oxford, UK. https://www.oclc.org/content/dam/research/events/2010/10-12d.pdf.

————. 2010b. "MPLP: It's Not Just for Processing Anymore." *American Archivist* 73: 175–203.

————. 2013. Untitled paper presented at annual meeting of The Society for the History of Authorship, Reading and Publishing, for the session "Digitization Crossroads."

————. 2015. "Acquisition Policy" in *Encyclopedia of Archival Science*, edited by Luciana Duranti and Patricia C. Franks, 9–12. Lanham, MD: Rowman and Littlefield.

Greene, Mark, and Dennis Meissner. 2005. "More Product, Less Process: Revamping Traditional Archival Processing." *American Archivist* 68: 208–263. http://archivists.metapress.com/content/c741823776k65863/fulltext.pdf.

Ham, F. Gerald. 1975. "The Archival Edge." *The American Archivist* 38: 5–13.

Jackson, Laura, and D. Thompson. 2010. "But You Promised: A Case Study of Deaccessioning at the American Heritage Center, University of Wyoming." *The American Archivist* 73: 669–685.

Janes, Robert. 2017. "Rethinking Museum Collections in a Troubled World." This volume.

Jones, Barbara. 2003. *Hidden Collections, Scholarly Barriers: Creating Access to Unprocessed Special Collections Material in North America's Libraries*. Association of Research Libraries Task Force on Special Collections. http://www.arl.org/storage/documents/publications/hidden-colls-white-paper-jun03.pdf.

Jonker, Agnes E. M. 2009. "No Privileged Past: Acquisition Revisited." *Journal of the Society of Archivists* 30(1): 67–80.

Marshall, Jennifer. 2002. "Toward Common Content: An Analysis of Online College and University Collecting Policies." *American Archivist* 65(2): 231–256.

Meissner, Dennis, and Mark A. Greene. 2010. "More Application while Less Appreciation: The Adopters and Antagonists of MPLP." *Journal of Archival Organization* 8(304): 174–226.

Online Computer Library Center. 2008. "Report of the WorldCat Local Special Collections and Archives Task Force." http://rbms.info/files/committees/bibliographic_standards/committee-docs/FinalReportWCLSpecCollTaskForce.pdf.

Sauer, Cynthia. 2001. "Doing the Best We Can? The Use of Collection Development Policies and Cooperative Collecting Activities at Manuscript Repositories." *American Archivist* 64(2): 308–349.

Schellenberg, Theodore R. 1956. *Modern Archives: Principles and Techniques*. Chicago: University of Chicago Press.

Shaw, George Bernard. 1903. *Man and Superman*. In *The Bodley Head Bernard Shaw: Collected Plays with Their Prefaces*, vol. 2, edited by Dan H. Laurence. London: Max Reinhardt, 1971.

Shelstad, Mark L. 1998. "Switching the Vacuum into Reverse: A Case Study of Retrospective Conversion as Collection Management." *Archival Issues* 23: 135–151.

Society of American Archivists. 2012. "Guidelines for Reappraisal and Deaccessioning." http://www2.archivists.org/sites/all/files/GuidelinesForReappraisalAndDeaccessioning-May2012.pdf.

Visser, Michelle. 2006. "Special Collections at ARL Libraries and K-12 Outreach: Current Trends." *The Journal of Academic Librarianship* 32(3): 313–319.

Vonnegut, Kurt. 1974. *The Sirens of Titan*. New York: Dell.

WE ARE COLLECTING *EMPTY* BOXES?

Elizabeth Wood, with Kayla Al Ameri

In a museum focused on hobbies like model building, preserving the joy and excitement of the process is as important as the objects themselves. Imagine for a moment perusing aisles and shelves of kits and packages of accessories and supplies for airplanes, rockets, railroads, or war games and thinking of all the amusement that comes from putting these models together. In the moment, that process is part and parcel of the objects and materials used. When the model building is complete, the end product serves as a reminder of the experience, from assembling the materials to putting the last touches on a finished model. How does a museum preserve that memory and experience? What physical remains of the process are most valuable to keep?

This is the question posed by Kayla Al Ameri, a museum studies graduate student, during her internship in one such museum. She was curious about the role of best practices in collections in small museums and came to discover an interesting problem. Boxes. Lots and lots of boxes. In the course of her internship activities she learned about the value and importance of saving the model boxes—the colorful and detailed exteriors can add to the overall story of each model. Most of the models in this museum however, were already assembled, many of them permanently, so lots of the model boxes were empty.

One box in particular posed a particular dilemma. The catalog record was incomplete for this box, it did not have a companion model, and it did not have anything inside it besides smaller, empty boxes. These empty boxes were for routine supplies like model glue, tape, and engine parts. Kayla pondered on this (Kayla Al Ameri, personal communication with the author, July 2016). She said,

> Given the intention behind the museum in wanting to preserve the joy and memories of model airplane building, history, and competition, I do not see the value in an empty box. Given limited resources, is there a

point to keeping empty boxes? Should it be done? Since I am all for active collections and purging museums of being packrats, I argue no. This is compounded by the fact that visitors tend to want the real thing. If they come in and see a box for a model and find out that the box is empty, the wow factor is depreciated.

To compound the problem even further, as part of her internship tasks, Kayla dutifully put the empty boxes into yet another archival box with a complete collections record.

The underlying problem for this box of empty boxes seems pretty clear. The empty containers shed no light on the model itself, they don't reveal or demonstrate the process of model building in a meaningful way, and at present they are taking up a cubic foot of space in a collection already bursting at the seams. Where is the bottom line for making decisions around what is and isn't serving the collection and the museum's mission? The empty box scenario seems like a good place to start.

The counter arguments (as we know well) would be:

1. The box and all the other empty boxes demonstrate the process—in its entirety—of making models as a hobby. The goal should be to have as comprehensive a record of this object as possible; thus they must be saved.
2. If we were doing an exhibit showing the process of how models are made, we might want to outline each step of the process. Since we don't know right now if we'll ever develop such an exhibit, we should keep this just in case.
3. We at least need the outside box, since that shows how the models were advertised and what the instructions were.
4. We cannot possibly know what future researchers might want to know about model airplanes. What if someone needs to study the glue or how the parts were punched out? How can we constrain future use by our present values?

These boxes and boxes and boxes serve as a classic example of how our field gets tangled up in "you never know when and how we might need this" and "when in doubt, save it," to the point that such instincts undermine common sense. Yes, there's some value in saving boxes, but it's a *relative* value, with significantly diminishing returns. The human meaning—the bliss of model-making—may lie in the promise of a just-opened kit, or the intricacies of the step-by-step challenge, or the triumph of a perfectly finished piece, but it is highly unlikely it lies in the pile of packaging left behind at the end of the project. What are the "boxes" in your collection, and what will it take for you to let them go?

7

RETHINKING MUSEUM COLLECTIONS IN A TROUBLED WORLD

Robert R. Janes

Budding Curation

My collecting started in early childhood and began with lead soldiers and expanded into natural history specimens. One of my stellar pieces was a gray whale vertebra—I used it as a stool in my bedroom and the neighborhood prestige it provided was unsurpassed. As did the oversized brain coral, the ivory walrus tusk, and the mounted gazelle skull with 18-inch horns. I frequented the back lanes of expensive homes with trash bins, the attics of our neighbors, and community bazaars. I was amazed to discover what people no longer wanted: a British World War I helmet, a wet bulb thermometer, an ancient Swiss-made pocket compass, and a four-inch ship in a bottle.

My collecting gene evolved, culminating in a 1930 Model A Coupe when I was 14. The fifty-dollar purchase price was easier to resolve than the parental support but this, too, materialized. I saw the coupe while scouting an unfamiliar neighborhood on my bike. The paint was gone, replaced by a powdery patina as the rust colonized the thick steel. The soft-top roof had collapsed and decayed into a mish-mash of rotting canvas and oak—you could sample it with a fork. The windowless interior was a ruptured mass of sodden woolen upholstery and chaotic springs. Worst of all, the trunk lid was gone, leaving a stark cavity in the otherwise curvaceous symmetry of the rear end. The open trunk was full of splintered oak boards, the archaeology of a low budget, pick-up truck conversion.

This thoughtless conversion was the most disturbing sign of entropy, and entropy has always been my bugbear. I suspect that's one reason why I've spent a lifetime in and around museums. Although I restored the coupe to mint condition, as an embryonic curator I was content to just let it sit and look good. Remember entropy: its silent partner is "use." My exotic collectible did not go unnoticed, and it prompted similar acquisitions among two of my teenage friends. All these things—lead soldiers, bones, army helmets, and Model As—needed care and attention. "If only they could talk," I often mused to myself. They didn't, so I made up my own stories to express my wonder and curiosity.

I still recall the only Nazi submarine ever captured during World War II, on exhibit at the Museum of Science and Industry in Chicago—*U-505.* I saw it when I was seven, and it is still there. The sub was set up to appear as if the crew had just jumped out of bed in a state of emergency, and the red and rumpled blankets are fixed in my memory. Or what about the suits of medieval armor in the Royal Ontario Museum in Toronto? I saw them when I was eight, and imagine how thrilled I was to have two full suits of armor as companions in my museum office 33 years later?

"If only things could talk," I continued to say to myself. Another encounter occurred on a fine July day in Canada's western subarctic. As a graduate student doing an archaeological survey of some abandoned cabins deep in the boreal forest, I noticed a small piston rod from an outboard motor, entangled in bearberry on the edge of an overgrown trail (Figure 7.1). This was a rare and unfamiliar piston rod, for not only was it broken, the shaft had also been repaired—tightly wrapped in green moose hide and then carefully bound in a coiled casing of brass snare wire. This ingenious repair was a pleasure to behold.

This object was a bold contradiction in my worldview, as a cracked piston rod is akin to a massive heart attack. Repair requires a specialist, and in the absence of such skill neither the rod nor the motor it powered has any further value. In the homeland of one of the world's greatest hunting cultures, the Dene hunter who presumably made this repair had no access to a machine shop or a mechanic,

FIGURE 7.1 Piston Rod, Photo Courtesy of Priscilla B. Janes

much less an outboard motor store.[1] In the absence of high organization and technological dependency, this nameless Dene saw possibilities and acted. Did this broken rod ever work again? Did this damage create a crisis in the unrelenting subarctic where tools are the necessity of life? Alive with questions and mystery, yet forever mute, is this not the wonder of objects? If only this object could talk.

With the benefit of hindsight, I now see that my childhood collecting, my training as an archaeologist in remote areas, my love of wilderness in all of its expressions, and my commitment to museums are multiple threads woven throughout my life experience. Although these threads are not discrete and linear pathways, they led to my eventual realization that we must acknowledge our "ecological selves"—the wider sense of identity that emerges when one's self-interest includes the natural world (Macy and Johnstone 2012, 94).

Encountering the Museum

With no prior museum experience and fresh from graduate school, I became the founding director of the Prince of Wales Northern Heritage Centre in Yellowknife, Northwest Territories (NWT), Canada in 1976. My interest in objects had persisted, and now embraced the material culture of the Aboriginal Peoples (Inuit, Dene, and Metis) who populated one of the most severe and immense wilderness regions in the world—Canada's north.[2] In the absence of the talking objects that I doggedly longed for, my education now came from the diverse peoples of the NWT and the land itself (Figure 7.2).

FIGURE 7.2   The Prince of Wales Northern Heritage Centre, Photo Courtesy of Wally Wolfe and the Prince of Wales Northern Heritage Centre

This cultural diversity, coupled with the severe climate and geographic isolation, posed a number of unexpected and bewildering challenges to me as a newly minted custodian of mainstream museum traditions. How do you address the stated perception among northern Aboriginal Peoples that museums and their collections are a colonial legacy and do not attend to the needs of living cultures? How do you involve Aboriginal Peoples in the development of a museum in their homeland, at a time when their political aspirations for self-determination were the priority? Are environmentally controlled museums in remote subarctic and Arctic communities necessary, achievable, or preposterous?

As convention dictates, the heart of the museum is the collection, and it was both my duty and belief to convey this tenet to northern communities. It soon became clear that many of the 65 NWT communities wanted a facility of some sort to preserve and highlight their cultural traditions, but not one that necessarily conformed to professional museum practice—that is, not with a permanent collection in an environmentally controlled building. The preservation and celebration of intangible cultural heritage—music, dance, and storytelling—were more often than not their real concerns, not the preservation of physical objects. Intangible cultural heritage has its own entropic forces in the NWT, including the mortality of wise elders and the relentless pressure of Euro-Canadian culture to consume and conform. Both were eroding or destroying traditional and local knowledge.

Here was a perspective on objects that denied not only my training, but also my own propensities as an undeclared curator. Mainstream museum practice dictated, however, that a publicly funded, community museum had to have environmental controls because without them the collections would deteriorate.

The residents of these remote communities were not interested in adhering to professional museum practice—not out of any disrespect or hostility, but because their worldview was fundamentally different. This worldview is best summed up by Eric Anoee, an Inuk Elder, who said, "We are not a materialistic people; we live by muscle, mind and spirit" (Heath 1997, 156). As a result of listening and learning together, we developed alternative approaches to museum work, while acknowledging museum traditions and professionalism (Janes 2016, 21–28, 29–39).

To fully understand and appreciate some of these alternatives, however, we had to abandon the traditional supposition that a museum must have a permanent collection. In retrospect, I see that we were challenging convention, although no one in the museum community but us was paying any attention. I note now that the absence of a permanent collection no longer spells heresy or incompetence, as "idea" museums are proliferating—one notable example being the new Canadian Museum for Human Rights in Winnipeg, where ideas, information, and knowledge, not objects, are the mainstay (see Canadian Museum for Human Rights: https://humanrights.ca/).

It was more useful to think of community museums in the Northwest Territories as preservers and purveyors of culture in its broadest sense, rather than as the repositories of material culture. Our evolving perspective was not

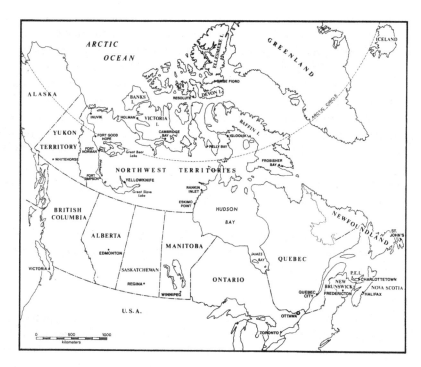

FIGURE 7.3 Map of the Northwest Territories, Image Courtesy of the Arctic Institute of North America

concerned with collections *per se*, but on reviving traditional values and technologies, and sharing them with the community at large. Because the cultures of northern Aboriginal Peoples are perpetuated by oral traditions, the knowledge and wisdom which brought objects into being are equally as worthy of preservation. This was a decade of listening and learning for me and as a result my unquestioned penchant for collecting unraveled and has never been restored. Nor do I feel the need for objects to speak to me. Individuals and communities do that now, along with their needs and their aspirations. I am now more likely to think of collections—or at least our dogged insistence in their primacy—as constraining the potential of museums.

Rethinking Collections

Others, too, have arrived in this no-man's-land where the *sine qua non* of museum practice—the permanent collection—is called into question. Hilary Jennings, director of the Happy Museum, posted the following comments on their website in response to the question, "Materialism degrades matter, can museums rise it up?"

The greatest opportunity for museums to lead Transition is to reshape the relationship between humans and objects. Unbridled economic growth has locked our identities to the things we possess. Our current individuality is shaped by what we own rather than the relationships we have with other people or our surroundings. As Happy Museum Founder, Tony Butler commented, "Museums have encouraged this. If they are not seduced by the glamour of treasure, they are overly concerned with narrative so that the sole purpose of objects is to tell a linear human story, invariably one of 'progress.'"

(Jennings 2015)

Bridget McKenzie (2011), museophile and cultural activist, put a finer point on the Happy Museum's concerns:

There is nothing, absolutely nothing, more important than that we face the fact that we have made our planet unliveable by our fetish for things. And what is a museum, fundamentally, other than a monument to our fetish for things?

There is both irony and paradox in the museum's fixation on material culture as a "linear story of progress." The reality is that individual museums are simply too bound by the inertia and expense of curatorial and institutional requirements to keep up with collecting the material culture of a society in process, even if they are overly concerned with the "glamour of treasure" and the story of progress. The complex nature of the curatorial process, including the procedures, the time, the energy, and the resources required, creates an internal inertia which few, if any, museums can overcome. This makes it mostly impossible for museum collections to reflect the dynamic nature of the society they claim to represent. If it is unrealistic to assume that this is achievable, are museums destined to be time capsules only—forever failing to embrace the continuum of time's arrow they are intended to serve?

If, indeed, museums are stuck in time, have they become the inadvertent ambassadors of the unbridled consumption that is unraveling the biosphere (Janes 2009b, 92–93)? In their celebration of materialism, have museums become the unwitting handmaidens to a value system that is at odds with our survival as a species? With unlimited collections growth and declining resources for collections care, coupled with an increasing emphasis on the marketplace, have museums lost their way? At a time of unprecedented socio-environmental challenges, are museums modeling the kind of behaviour that succeeding generations require of us?

I cannot help but return to my silent epiphany in the boreal forest mentioned earlier, light years distant from the heedless consumption that defines contemporary life and museum collecting. Life and death in the boreal forest have always hinged on the appropriate tools, and being able to care for them. Someone had made the repair to the piston rod while attuned to this imperative by using "muscle, mind, and spirit." It was impossible to tell if the repair had worked and if the broken rod had once again served its purpose. It doesn't matter. What matters is putting context to that object and the imagined story, a context that is value-based, instructive, and inspired by our collective intelligence to help create a new, caring, sustainable, and more conscious future for ourselves, our communities, and the planet.

What also matters is the museum's responsibility to continually question—to reject complacency and the status quo, and to juxtapose and consider disparate values, worldviews, and aspirations. This is why we have museums, why people value them, and why people work in them. The piston rod was a lesson in how objects matter outside the method and theory of museum practice. Are museum collections contributing to our collective intelligence in ways that matter outside their own walls? Are museums supporting the numinous experience with objects that are grounded in the fortunes, challenges, and calamities of individuals, families, and communities? We need to set aside our professional servitude to collections for collections' sake and think more deeply about their use in creating personal meaning and collective wisdom.

In Search of the Numinous

Nurturing the numinous perspective begins with us acknowledging our "ecological selves" as mentioned earlier—the wider sense of identity that emerges when one's self-interest includes the natural world (Macy and Johnstone 2012, 94). Put another way, we must embrace the meaning of social ecology—that social and environmental issues are intertwined and both must be considered simultaneously (Barnhill 2010, 91). To put it yet another way, we must find our way to a numinous—or sacred—relationship with both the natural world and each other. The numinous experience is under siege, however, at a time when our highly technological, interconnected, global civilization is also threatened with collapse by an array of environmental problems (Ehrlich and Ehrlich 2013, 1). Consider this observation from John Greer, an ecological historian. He summed up our human predicament this way:

> Most ordinary people in the industrial world . . . are sleepwalking through one of history's great transitions. The issues that concern them are still defined entirely by the calculus of abundance . . . It has not yet entered their darkest dreams that they need to worry about access to such basic necessities as food . . . or the fate of local economies and communities shredded by decades of malign neglect, or the rise of serious threats to the survival of constitutional government and the rule of law.
>
> *(Greer 2011, 239)*

More specifically, we must now contend with the accelerating extinction of animal and plant populations upon which we depend, including the dramatic decline of the world's fisheries; an 80% loss of the planet's forest cover; the spread of toxic compounds; and the use of environmentally damaging technologies, such as fracking for oil and gas, to maintain our unbridled consumption (Voice of America 2013; World Wildlife Fund 2016; World Preservation Foundation 2010).

Are museums and their collections helping to protect this vital relationship with our ecological selves?

The forging of an ecology of museums is long overdue—an ecology that recognizes that a broad web of societal relationships is the only way for museums to sustain themselves. This inescapable interdependence is the harbinger of a new future for museums, as museums of all kinds are untapped and untested sources of ideas and knowledge. They are ideally placed to foster individual and community participation in the quest for greater awareness and workable solutions to our global problems. As deeply trusted social institutions in civil society, museums are essential in fostering public support of decisive and immediate action to address our human predicament.

It is clear that museums are not meant to solve climate change or any other global problems, but museums *are* in a position to invent a new future for themselves and their communities. Museums can at least help create an image of a desirable future—the essential first step in its realization. The world also needs museums that provide cultural frameworks to identify and challenge the myths and misperceptions that threaten all of us—such as the preposterous notion that continuous economic growth is the key to our well-being. Public dialogue on economic growth in a world of dire environmental constraints is long overdue. There are clearly limits to growth and all museums, as well as all of our public institutions, must now consider just how invasive the reigning model of unlimited growth and consumption has become, and change direction.

Mindful Curation

How, then, might museums and their collections make meaningful contributions to these global challenges? By repositioning themselves in the service of human ecology, broadly and holistically conceived. For one, museums are the only social institution with a three-dimensional, cultural memory bank, representing material diversity and adaptive intelligence. If seed banks are gene banks of biodiversity, then museums are tool, technology, history, and art banks—curating the most distinctive trait of our species—the ability to make tools and things of beauty (Janes 2009b, 179). Museums are also the repositories of our adaptive failures and successes, as well as our creativity (Janes 2016, 250). In this sense, museums are akin to the biological seed banks that store seeds as a source for planting, in case seed reserves elsewhere are destroyed.

Modernity has led to the loss of knowledge about sustainable-living practices that have guided our species for millennia, and museums will be a fundamental source of technological memory, as solutions are sought for failed technology. The need to revisit this cumulative knowledge from the past is necessary now, as industrial technology becomes increasingly maladaptive. Moreover, museums contain our civilization's most comprehensive catalog of *both* cultural and natural diversity. Should the worst come to pass and the world plunges into some variant of an apocalyptic or post-apocalyptic scenario, and if museums survive, they may find themselves playing an essential stewardship role in which some collections serve as guides to rebuilding sustainable societies. As author James Kunstler (2005, 130) asks:

> If the social and economic platform fails, how long before the knowledge base dissolves? Two hundred years from now, will anyone know how to build or even repair a 1962 Chrysler slant-six engine? Not to mention a Nordex 1500 kW wind turbine?

The concept of museums as seed banks goes beyond the objects themselves, to include the local and traditional knowledge that resides not only in the objects, but also in the written and oral testimony that accompanies them. We have come full circle to the adaptive genius of my northern Aboriginal mentors discussed earlier. Above all, it was the knowledge and the spirit that motivated them—the artifact was the offspring—impressive but not time tested as wisdom is. All of these forms of knowledge are currently under siege, for "as knowledge expands globally, it is being lost locally," writes Wendell Berry (2000, 90–91). He notes that "modern humans typically are using places whose nature they have never known and whose history they have forgotten; thus ignorant, they almost necessarily abuse what they use."

Every museum, irrespective of size and subject, can make this connection between the collections and knowledge they hold, and the issues and challenges that confront society now. To do so, museums must move beyond the conventions of entertainment, popularity, and ancillary education, and start examining the compelling, societal questions that are shaping the future. These are the questions that bind us together as members of the human family and pave the path toward an ecology of museums.

The most compelling societal question is how our civilization will respond to climate change. If the biosphere unravels because of catastrophic climate change, there will be no other issues of consequence as the planet Earth is our only life support system. Fortunately, it is now recognized that natural history collections in museums and research institutions are a valuable resource for climate change research. In a recent article in *BioScience*, the authors noted that "natural history collections hold billions of specimens collected over the past two centuries, each potentially witness to past ecological conditions and irrefutable evidence of historical biogeographic distributions" (Johnson et al. 2011, 147). The multiple authors of this article, most of whom work in museums, call for a strategic realignment among holders of natural history collections to expand their existing focus on taxonomy and systematics—with climate change as a priority. They also note that setting these new priorities will require strong partnerships between collection holders and global change biologists (Johnson et al. 2011). This is a cogent example of conscious museum workers who are rethinking the role and responsibilities of their collections to meet a changing and troubled world. Inevitably, they will have to broaden their collaboration to include consumers, media, business, government, and educational organizations if this work is to have a substantive impact.

Another example of museums rethinking their relationship to social ecology is taking place at the Western Development Museum in Saskatchewan, Canada. This institution not only installed wind turbines to help offset its utility costs, but also created an exhibition that publicly monitors the performance of the wind turbines while featuring the pioneering innovations of early prairie farmers to capture the wind (Janes 2009a).

Beyond the walls of the museum, meanwhile, there is a profound opportunity for nurturing a no-growth economy that integrates public advocacy, problem solving, collaboration, accountability, and the museum as seed bank—in a coalition of nonprofit organizations and businesses called a Community Economic Laboratory, or CEL (Heinberg 2011, 276–278). This coalition provides a variety of services, ranging from individual learning to community involvement, and could include a food cooperative, a community garden, a tool library, a work centre to match people's skills with community needs, a recycling centre, and a community education centre, as well as a museum or gallery with all of its unique resources and services.

There is also another initiative of immediate relevance to museums—the Global Village Construction Set or GVCS (Open Source Ecology 2016). The goal of this project is to provide access to basic technology needed for a sustainable and locally self-sufficient existence in communities. The GVCS is inventing open-source blueprints that enable the fabrication of 50 key industrial machines from readily available, recycled materials. There is certainly room for museums in this creative enterprise, recognizing that preservation, knowledge, and access are key features of both the GVCS and museums. A partnership of some sort could result in a hybrid museum—wherein the museum's collection is used to generate goods, services, and income for both the museum and the collective good.

I cannot overstate that museums are unique social institutions, given their larger view of time. With this in mind, consider the question of Macy and Johnstone: "for how long would we like our family to continue? If the next generation matters to us, and the children born to it do as well, then what about their children, and their children's children?" (Macy and Johnstone 2012, 142). Museums are predisposed to exercise their larger view of time as stewards of the biosphere, and can harness their unparalleled understanding of stewardship to serve the human family more holistically. This is the context for material culture that fills me with excitement and purpose now, as the whale vertebra and the 1930 Model A Coupe did so many years ago.

Conclusions

It is essential at this point in history for museum workers to suspend their conventional opinions about what meaningful museum work is and, instead, consider what the work of museums should be in the early twenty-first century. There are acute issues confronting our species that require concerted public involvement with the aid of intelligent social organizations like museums. For mindful museums with a true sense of stewardship, one immediate challenge is to assess their collections to determine what is essential and valuable to save in advance of a low energy future and the cessation of unlimited economic growth. Another is to assess how collections can support social ecology.

The idea of museums as seed banks is perhaps the strongest endorsement for museums to participate in defining a future divorced from economic growth—both as stewards and as disseminators of a historical consciousness in support of rethinking contemporary assumptions and misperceptions. If historical consciousness can be defined "as a form of resourcefulness in using historical data as 'material' to make sense of our world," then museums are the embodiment of that consciousness (Gosselin 2012, 197). This is an obvious role for museums in a troubled world.

The museum's historical consciousness can be at play in the present by embracing community issues and aspirations that will help make sense of the challenges we face, not only in the approach to exhibitions and public programming but also in the approach to collections. All museums are key agents in fostering the societal transition from the doomed economy of industrial growth to the recognition that the numinous connection between individuals, communities, and nature is essential to our collective well-being (Korten 2014).

As the poet/farmer Wendell Berry (2015, 71) succinctly noted, "If we are serious about these big problems, we have got to see that the solutions begin and end with ourselves. Thus we put an end to our oversimplification." I am hoping that museum workers are ready and able to become serious about the meaning and value of their collections, within the context of the big problems that Berry mentions. We know what those big problems are, be they climate change, environmental degradation, or the inevitability of depleted fossil fuels, not to mention racism, poverty, and migration. Museum collections can be part of big problems, or they can be part of big solutions when managed with mindfulness and foresight.

Will the keepers of collections continue to use their collections for reasons of learned self-interest and aesthetic appeal, or will they use them to enhance the durability and well-being of individuals and communities? Can we put an end to our oversimplification, as Berry hopes? There is a choice. There need not be an apocalypse for the benefits of the museum's unique form of stewardship to be reaped. The museum community can embrace an uncertain future by changing how it thinks and works, collections included. Be it the thrill of collecting as a child and a curator, or honouring the profound interconnectedness between nature and culture—objects, culture, and nature make us human. Museums must safeguard this hallowed triad and all that it signifies.

Acknowledgements

I am indebted to Elee Wood, Rainey Tisdale, and Trevor Jones for inviting me to participate in the Active Collections project. I thank each of them for their guidance and support. This essay contains material from some of my earlier writings on collections and museum management—extracted, revised, and updated accordingly. Please see the citations and references for details. I acknowledge the original sources of this material, particularly my publisher, Routledge.

Notes

1 The Dene people (DEN-ay) are an aboriginal group of First Nations who live in the northern boreal and subarctic regions of Canada. Denendeh means "The Land of the People," and is located in the Northwest Territories, Canada.
2 Inuit are the Aboriginal people of Arctic Canada, and the Metis are descendants of people born of relations between First Nations women and European men.

References

Ainslie, Patricia. 2001. "A Collection for the Millennium: Grading the Collections at Glenbow." *Museum Management and Curatorship* 19(1): 93–104.

Barnhill, David Landis. 2010. "Gary Snyder's Ecosocial Buddhism." In *How Much Is Enough? Buddhism, Consumerism, and the Human Environment*, edited by Richard K. Payne, 83–110. Somerville, MA: Wisdom Publications.

Berry, Wendell. 2000. *Life is a Miracle*. Berkeley, CA: Counterpoint.

———. 2015. *Our Only World*. Berkeley, CA: Counterpoint.

Ehrlich, Paul R., and Anne H. Ehrlich. 2013. "Can a Collapse of Global Civilization be Avoided?" *Proceedings of the Royal Society B* 280(1754): 20122845, 1–9. http://rspb.royal societypublishing.org/content/280/1754/20122845.full.pdf+html.

Gosselin, Vivianne. 2011. "Open to Interpretation: Mobilizing Historical Thinking in the Museum." PhD diss., University of British Columbia. https://open.library.ubc.ca/cIRcle/collections/ubctheses/24/items/1.0055355.

Greer, John Michael. 2011. *The Wealth of Nature*. Gabriola Island, Canada: New Society Publishers.

Heath, Terrence. 1997. "Comments from Afar." In *Museums and the Paradox of Change: A Study in Urgent Adaptation*, 2nd edition, edited by Robert R. Janes. Calgary, Canada: Glenbow Museum and the University of Calgary Press.

Heinberg, Richard. 2011. *The End of Growth: Adapting to Our New Economic Reality*. Gabriola Island, Canada: New Society Publishers.

———. 2015. *Afterburn: Society Beyond Fossil Fuels*. Gabriola Island, Canada: New Society Publishers.

Janes, Robert R. 2009a. "It's a Jungle in Here: Museums and Their Self-Inflicted Challenges." *MUSE* 27(5): 30–33.

———. 2009b. *Museums in a Troubled World: Renewal, Irrelevance or Collapse?* London and New York: Routledge.

———. 2013. *Museums and the Paradox of Change*, 3rd edition. London and New York: Routledge.

———. 2016. *Museums without Borders: Selected Writings of Robert R. Janes*. London and New York: Routledge.

Jennings, Hilary. 2015. "Materialism Degrades Matter, Can Museums Rise it Up?" *The Happy Museum*. http://happymuseumproject.org/materialism-degrades-matter-can-museums-rise/.

Johnson, Kenneth G., Stephen J. Brooks, Phillip B. Fenberm, Adrian G. Glover, Karen E. James, Adrian M, Lister, Ellinor Michel, Mark Spencer, Jonathan A. Todd, Eugenia Valsami-Jones, Jeremy R. Young, and John R. Stewart. 2011. "Climate Change and Biosphere Response: Unlocking the Collections Vault." *BioScience* 61(2): 147–153.

Keene, Suzanne. 2005. *Fragments of the World: Uses of Museum Collections*. Oxford: Elsevier Butterworth-Heinemann.

Korten, David C. 2014. "Change the Story, Change the Future: A Living Economy for a Living Earth." Presentation at the Praxis Peace Institute Conference, San Francisco, California, October 7. http://livingeconomiesforum.org/sites/files/pdfs/David%20Korten%20Praxis%20Peace%20Oct%207%202014%20for%20distribution.pdf.

Kunstler, James Howard. 2005. *The Long Emergency: Surviving the End of Oil, Climate Change, and Other Converging Catastrophes of the Twenty-First Century*. New York: Grove Press.

Macy, Joanna, and Chris Johnstone. 2012. *Active Hope: How to Face the Mess We're in Without Going Crazy*. Novato, CA: New World Library.

McKenzie, Bridget. 2011. "The Climate Crisis and the 'Happy Museum.'" *The Learning Planet*. https://thelearningplanet.wordpress.com/2011/08/29/the-climate-crisis-and-the-happy-museum/.

Open Source Ecology. 2016. *The Global Village Construction Set*. http://opensourceecology.org/.

O'Riordan, Jon and Robert William Sandford. 2015. *The Climate Nexus*. Victoria, Canada: Rocky Mountain Books.

Romm, Joe. 2013. "Into the Valley of Death Rode the 600, Into the Valley of 400 PPM Rode the 7 Billion." *Think Progress*. May 5. https://thinkprogress.org/into-the-valley-of-death-rode-the-600-into-the-valley-of-400-ppm-rode-the-7-billion-2534f767bb75.

Thompson, Keith. 1998. "Museums: Dilemmas and Paradoxes." *American Scientist* 86(6): 520.

Voice of America. 2013. "Tree Bark Shows Global Spread of Toxic Chemicals." http://www.voanews.com/content/tree_bark_shows_global_spread_of_toxic_chemicals/1622579.html.

World Preservation Foundation. 2010. "Deforestation Statistics." http://www.worldpreservationfoundation.org/blog/news/deforestation-statistics/#.UxZH67mYZKo.

World Wildlife Fund. 2016. "Overfishing." http://worldwildlife.org/threats/overfishing.

Worts, Douglas. 2008. "Rising to the Challenge: Fostering a Culture of Sustainability." *MUSE* 26: 6.

ACTIVATE YOUR OBJECT

51 Questions to Reveal Inactivity

Katherine Rieck

In 1982, John Hennigar Shuh wrote the well-loved essay, "Teaching Yourself to Teach with Objects," in which he made a list of "50 Ways to Look at a Big Mac Box." Questions ranged from "What material was used to make this object?" to "Taste it" (Shuh 1982, 89–90). Shuh's groundbreaking list encouraged museum professionals to think beyond a standard description of an object and literally look at the object in 50 different ways. Although it takes time to ask all of these questions of any object, the real goal is to train your brain in a way of thinking or questioning how to better "activate" your collection.

This following list is the Active Collections version of Shuh's "50 Ways to Look at a Big Mac Box." Inspired by ideas and themes from the essays in this volume, these questions will help you explore the hidden assumptions, potential connections, and missed opportunities that the conventional object record overlooks. And, there's a bonus question to keep it all in perspective.

Value

1. Is it visually interesting?
2. How does the object's condition affect its ability to be active?
3. Could the object be put on display? If so, for how long?
4. Could people handle or use it?
5. What is the cost of gaining intellectual control of this object, taking into consideration staff time and materials for research, cataloging, and inventory?
6. What is the cost of preserving this object, taking into account conservation, housing materials, climate-controlled storage, and staff time, for a month? A year? A decade?
7. Is this object worth its carbon footprint?
8. Does your museum have the resources to digitalize this object?
9. How would that digitalization change the object experience?

The Object and Your Collection

10. Does your institution own multiples of this object?
11. Is a duplicate of this object in other institutions' collections?
12. How does this object support your current collecting scope?
13. How does this object support your institution's mission?
14. Where does this object fit into your collection? Is it merely filling a gap within an encyclopedic collection? Does it illuminate a human story?
15. How does this object align within the interpretive goals of your institution today? What is your education staff's perspective on its interpretive value?
16. Does this object fit more with the "here and now" of your institution or with the undetermined future?
17. Who accepted the donation/purchase of this object? Why?
18. What was the collecting vision of your institution when this object was acquired? Has the collecting vision changed since then, and if so, how?
19. Who is the donor of this object? Did they donate other items to your institution as well? What were the donor's motivations? What does this donor history reveal about your museum as a collecting institution?
20. What does the donation record reveal about the object? About your greater community?

Uncovering the Meaning of the Object

21. Was this object mass-produced?
22. What is this object's unique human story?
23. What other uses or purposes did this object have beyond its original intended use?
24. Does this object reinforce racial, gender, class, or other stereotypes? How so?
25. What do these stereotypes reveal about your institution? Your community? Your collecting policy?
26. Is this object commonly associated with people of privilege? Can it be used to help your public audiences explore and question systems of privilege?

Representation

27. What need in your communities does this object fill?
28. Where could you place this object in your communities?
29. What interpretations would that placement reveal?
30. Is there a community organization or group that you could loan this object to?
31. What potential connections or new life could this object have within this community organization?
32. How could this object serve the public outside the museum walls?
33. Could your communities be brought together by this object's interpretation? By its destruction?
34. Would this object—and your communities—be better served if the museum did not own it?

Interpretation

35. Does this object evoke sensory experiences, memories, emotions, or universal human themes? What potential interpretive strategies do such connections reveal about the object?
36. How many humans have had contact with this object?
37. Aside from actual contact, what are the broader human connections to this object?
38. How could this object be used to illustrate a person's story?
39. Who could relate to those stories?
40. Who couldn't relate to those stories?
41. Could another object in your collection tell these stories better?
42. What community's stories could be highlighted with this object?
43. What individual, ethnic groups, or community groups could participate in the interpretation of this object?
44. How would these groups interpret the object?
45. In what way could visitors interact with this object?
46. How could you situate this object so that it would inspire an "aha moment"?
47. In what ways could the stereotypes implied by this object be used to share stories of the current time or the historical past?
48. Could this object inspire visitors to grow in their relationships with their own objects?
49. What sort of relationship with objects is your museum modeling with this object? Hoarding? Perpetual preservation? Acknowledging the natural life cycle of collections?
50. Beyond display, is there another way that your institution could use this object? Could this object be given away to serve a greater purpose? Allowed to decay?

And finally . . .

51. Why is this object still in your collection?

Reference

Shuh, John Hennigar. 1999. "Teach Yourself to Teach With Objects." In *The Educational Role of the Museum*, 2nd edition, edited by Eilean Hooper-Greenhill, 80–91. London: Routledge.

SECTION II

New Ideas and Tools for Change

FIGURE 0.2A   Image by Ray Rieck (www.rayrieck.com)

8

TIER YOUR COLLECTIONS

A Practical Tool for Making Clear Decisions in Collections Management

Trevor Jones

Imagine that in your museum's collection there is a sword that was given by prominent citizens to a Union soldier during the Civil War because he defied President Lincoln's orders to enlist African American troops. The sword is a symbol of the racial fault lines in that community, the state, and the entire nation. Also in the collection is a Model 1850 Staff and Field Officer's sword. It is unclear where it came from or who used it, and you have seven others just like it in the collection. Are these artifacts equal? If they are not, should you give them the same standard of care?

With large and diverse collections it can be difficult to separate the significant from the mundane. Many museums have collections spanning decades with levels of provenance ranging from detailed portfolios to "drop offs" that made their way into the collection without documentation. I've spent much of my career working in state historical societies, and managing a long-standing collection spanning the entire state from prehistory to the present is challenging. To deal with these issues I've been experimenting with ways to sort collections based on how well they support the mission. Assigning a tier or rank to each item or collection helps easily distinguish the wheat from the chaff.

Tiering Your Collections

In graduate school I was trained to treat every object in my museum as if they were all equally valuable. As Jim Vaughn wrote in 2008, museum workers have been traditionally asked to "treat every object as if it were a Rembrandt" (Vaughn, 33). The idea that all collections are equal sounds fair, but the reality is very different. If you've worked with collections, you know that significant items are, in fact, not treated the same as the others. The best security and display cases are often reserved for important collections, and most disaster plans feature a list of "the good stuff" that should be rescued first. There's always a difference between theory and practice, but the "Rembrandt Rule" (Vaughn, 2008) concept actually inhibits our ability to make collections come alive for our audiences. Because theory says all collections are equal, the idea of creating a formalized triage system and using it to improve collections management is rarely openly discussed.

When I worked at the Kentucky Historical Society, we began ranking our collections into different tiers of use and experienced some surprising results. Ranking resulted in better treatment for significant collections, conserved scarce resources, and even began to change how our staff and board think about the "value" of our collections. Unused collections benefit no one, and ranking them by importance to the mission helps ensure that we collect only those things that can effectively engage our audiences. Ranking collections officially acknowledges what we already know but don't talk about—that some collections are more useful than others and not everything is a Rembrandt.

Tiering (or ranking) of museum collections is not new. It has existed for years, primarily at living history museums. These museums focus on interpreting a living past, and developed ranking systems that would allow them to use artifacts in interpretive programs. Institutions such as the Henry Ford have tiered their collections to rank objects into categories: pieces that can be touched or operated until destroyed, artifacts that should be used only infrequently, and ones that should not be handled at all (see Fahey and Deck, 2001). This method remains an effective way to create different ranks for collections based on how they will be used. The University of Oxford's Bate Collection of Musical Instruments has used a similar grid system for years to rank instruments according to their rarity and how likely they are to be damaged by use. The two scores on the grid are added together to determine if the instrument can be played (see Lamb, 2007). Other organizations have used tiers (or grades) to rank their collections based on considerations that take aesthetics into account. The Speed Art Museum in Louisville, Kentucky graded their art collection based on each piece's "artistic quality, condition, and art historical significance" (personal conversation with Kim Spence of the Speed Art Museum, April 29, and email on July 1, 2016).

I believe tiering efforts are most effective when the core criteria are determined by and closely tied to the institutional mission. At the Kentucky Historical Society, the mission is to "educate and engage the public through Kentucky's history in order to confront the challenges of the future." It follows that the collections (and indeed everything the organization does) should be judged by how well it supports that mission. Anchoring collections to the mission helps ensure they can play an active role in supporting the museum's programs. In Kentucky we began our ranking project by convening the Collections Committee to discuss how well our collections were currently supporting the mission.

This initial discussion was sometimes contentious, but it helped clarify previously unspoken assumptions and shed light on how different departments viewed the role of collections. After several conversations, it was clear that the core question we wanted to ask of every single collection is: "How can this help tell stories about Kentucky's past that will be meaningful to Kentuckians today and in the future?" Defining this question gave voice to two of our shared beliefs—that collections

TABLE 8.1 Criteria for Tiering Collections

Tier 1	Tier 2	Tier 3	Tier 4	Tier 5
Significant to Kentucky AND nationally or internationally significant	Significant historical value to Kentucky. Strong provenance	Historical value to a location in Kentucky. Limited provenance	Historical value to other locations, no Kentucky connection	Limited or no historical value. Limited or no provenance
Few, if any duplicates in this or other collections and/or of high monetary value	Few similar examples in this or other collections	Similar examples are held in this or other collections	Common in this or other collections	
Rare, likely irreplaceable	Uncommon and difficult to replace	Moderately difficult to replace	NA	NA
Could be used to tell multiple powerful stories about Kentucky and its place in the nation	Could be used to tell multiple powerful stories about the state	Plays a supporting role in telling stories about the state	May play a supporting role or illustrate a concept, but is not the focus	Plays a minor role
Example: Doram paintings—two wealthy free people of color. Deep provenance.	Example: Wm. J. Goebel's coat—assassinated state governor. Used as trial evidence.	Example: Copper still—made in small town in eastern part of the state. Confiscated in Prohibition.	Example: Flapper dress. Great condition—acquired by Los Angeles costume designer.	Example: Woodworking planes acquired by a collector. Over 400 of them with no other info.

should be used, and that provenance is the key factor in determining a collection's importance to the organization. Condition, function, and aesthetics all play a role in ranking collections, but for us a collection's ability to illuminate a story from the state's past is the element that truly matters. As a result, a rare Stickley settle in perfect condition with no provenance to the state will always be less important to the mission than a battered, mass-produced sofa purchased by a Kentucky family and used in their home in Paducah.

Once we had agreed on criteria, it was possible to create a preliminary tiering grid (Table 8.1), but the process did not start smoothly. We initially struggled because ranking collections is a subjective process and it feels uncomfortable at first. Deciding that some things are more important than others goes against years of collections training, as well as a desire not to pass judgment on an artifact without knowing every possible fact. Our team felt they were not qualified to judge specific collections, and pushed to be allowed to bring in experts to look at specific items. I spent time in the early days explaining that giving a collection a low rank doesn't mean it is "bad," it is just less useful in supporting our museum's mission. Lower-ranked collections are sometimes both wonderful and rare, but they are ranked lower because they are less able to support our research and programming. In the grid, it's the top level that carries the most weight for making a determination. Significant provenance connected to the mission typically outweighs quantity or rarity.

Like many classroom teachers, we found that it's not that complicated to award the best and worst grades—but figuring out the difference between a B and a C is agonizing. The most important pieces in a collection are pretty easy to rank (if you work with a collection you probably can create a solid list off the top of your head right now), and collections that don't belong in your museum are also easy to list. However, choosing what belongs in Tier 3 can be a trial. In 2014 one of our curators started tiering artifacts and shared her issues with the mid-range artifacts:

> We have a variety of items that have Kentucky connections or a decent provenance—But is a mass produced vase owned by a Kentuckian as important as a regionally significant carver's woodworking tools? What about a quilt made by an enslaved person in western Kentucky versus the Cherry Blossom Queen's dress which was worn by a non-Kentuckian who represented the state in the Cherry Blossom Festival?

These are good questions, and questions around artifacts of local or regional significance will always be the most challenging.

However, tiering is a collections management tool, and it is often best used by looking at the collection as a whole. When you break down the Kentucky Historical Society's results, it's clear that Tier 3 is by far the largest category, consisting of over 55% of ranked objects. Tier 1 is the smallest at 1.9%, Tier 2 has nearly 8%, Tier 4 has 20%, and Tier 5 has 14%. It is encouraging that over two-thirds of the entire collection has a definite connection to the mission, but for a state historical society, it's disheartening that more of it can't tell a strong state story. Tiers 4 and 5 account for more than a third of the total collection, and these artifacts are either "type" pieces with no real provenance, or do not fit the mission at all. In aggregate, tiering shows there are a large number of artifacts that do not actively support the mission. Although most organizations will likely need at least some collections in all of the first four tiers, the distribution across these areas shows that time and money is being spent caring for too many unneeded objects.

Tiering Isn't the Same as Creating a Deaccession List

Although tiering helps make deaccessioning decisions, this method of collection ranking is not in itself a deaccessioning tool. "Tier 5" ranking is reserved for collections that have nothing whatsoever to do with the mission ("Why exactly do we have twenty-seven Portuguese bayonets with absolutely no provenance?"), but not everything that needs to be deaccessioned will fit in Tier 5. The Kentucky Historical Society has thousands of items that support the mission, but are also duplicates. The Society has an excellent political collection, but does it really need eight copies of the same bumper sticker from a 1986 state judicial election? As they have local significance, placing the duplicates in Tier 5 would be wrong, but there still needs to be a way to indicate that seven bumper stickers need to go.

To solve this, a separate "Deaccession/Yes/No" field needs to be created. That way the duplicate bumper stickers could be tagged as Tier 3 (local significance), but also tagged "Yes" in the deaccession field. This simple method allows staff to sort by both tier and the deaccession tag to create disposal priorities. Creating the deaccession field makes it easy to allow anyone working with collections to recommend an item or collection for deaccessioning. At the Kentucky Historical Society, volunteers and interns were encouraged to tag any item for deaccessioning if it was a duplicate or if they could not determine its benefit. These people may not be trained curators, but they know the collection, and it's inefficient not to give them the power to recommend disposing of some of the items they come across when opening cabinet drawers. The Collections Committee still retains authority to recommend items for deaccessioning to the board, but this cannot be done if they don't know it's there. The basic "Deaccession/Yes/No" tag provides a solid starting point for making these decisions on disposal priorities.

At the Kentucky Historical Society, tiering has not been a perfect solution but it has improved collections management. The process illuminated gaps in the collections, and new focus areas where the organization needs to actively solicit collections that support the mission. Disaster planning was simplified, as tiering makes it easy to create a comprehensive list of Tier 1 collections that should be rescued first in the event of a disaster. These benefits could have been anticipated, but others were more surprising. The tiering system also helped staff reconsider how artifacts are stored.

As in many museums, the Kentucky Historical Society's storage space is mostly filled by artifacts that are in a drawer or cabinet because they were the first to be cataloged. This means some significant artifacts are stored in second-rate storage areas. Flat storage spaces for flags were full, but funding for new cabinets was unavailable. However, many flags with no provenance (Tier 4) were taking up valuable space in the best cabinets. The solution was to work to remove these lower-tier artifacts and switch them with higher-tier items, so the best storage could be used for artifacts that best support the mission. Tiering can help change how collections managers think about how best to use their available resources to support their collections.

Finally, ranking collections in this manner changed the Kentucky Historical Society's conversations about artifacts in more subtle ways. Tiering levels were added to Collections Committee documents so that anyone recommending a potential acquisition on a donation assessment form could be expected to assign a tier as part of their recommendation. Although compliance was hit-and-miss, adding tiers focused committee discussions more concretely about how an acquisition would actively support the mission. Starting the conversation with "how will we use this?" prompts staff to convince the committee to say yes to the acquisition, rather than forcing them to find reasons to say no. Saying no to donors is never easy, but by ranking the collections, the committee is less likely to accept a collection that won't actively support the mission. The first step to maximizing the use of your collections is to stop taking in things you do not need, and tiering collections can help with that process.

BOX 8.1   Tips for Creating Your Own Tiering or Ranking System

- Tie your criteria directly to the mission. Your collections should support what your museum is there to do. If you aren't judging your collections on how they support the mission, chances are they'll never be much use to your organization.
- Don't worry about creating a perfect system. The key to this process is to start and adapt it as needed. If you wait until you have everything perfect, you'll never get off the ground.
- You don't need to be an expert to rank most collections. Knowing something about your collection definitely helps, but in many cases it will be easy to tell if an artifact supports your mission. Don't get paralyzed by the fear of what you don't know.
- Good curators and strong documentation will definitely improve your project. Curatorial expertise and provenance in the files will increase confidence in the system. At the Kentucky Historical Society, the original hope was to tier our artifacts during inventory but it was too time consuming to look at accession records and reference books. Tiering instead became part of the cataloging process in order to make the best use of our institutional knowledge.
- Tiering is not a substitute for a deaccessioning plan.[1] Tiering will help determine what needs to be deaccessioned, but you'll still want to mark items for deaccession in a separate field so that you can eliminate duplicates.
- Distribute the responsibility. Make use of the knowledge and expertise of anyone (especially volunteers) who works with collections. Encourage

their input into the process. If it's not clear to your volunteers why something is there, it's not going to be clear to anyone else.

- Don't get bogged down in the middle rankings! Tiering is a collections management system and is designed to help you see patterns and assist in planning. The difference between the middle grades is not that important overall.

---

1 It changed again in 2014, but I like the National Trust's earlier definition of deaccessioning: "to deaccession an object is to formally and permanently remove it from the collections. To dispose of an object is to relinquish title and remove the object from the premises" (Anderson, 235).

It is also possible that there are other benefits from tiering that are yet to be realized. Tiering could be used to change how we loan artifacts to other museums, in order to make it easier for institutions to borrow lower tiered collections with minimal restrictions. In this type of system, borrowing a Tier 1 item would still require a facilities report, but borrowing a Tier 4 collection would require only a one-page form and no security. This approach would open the loan program to a wider variety of museums, and increase sharing of collections. My dream is to someday see a system similar to interlibrary loan for museums where it's easy to borrow common "type pieces" and so that every history museum would no longer feel the need to own multiple examples of spinning wheels and butter churns. That's a long way off, but perhaps by making it easier to borrow artifacts that are not precious to us, we can encourage communication and cooperation among museums.

I encourage you to develop your own ranking system for your museum's collections. Museums have diverse missions, so yours will look different if your museum's mission is different—and that's great! Tiering can help you manage your collections more efficiently, but the end goal is to help your collections more actively support your museum's mission.

References

Fahey, Mary, and Clara Deck. 2001. "Responsibilities, Realities and Ranking: How a Collections Tiering Policy Aids Conservators in Ethical Decision Making and Judicious Resource Allocation at the Henry Ford Museum and Deerfield Village." *Objects Specialty Group Postprints* 8: 97–105.

Lamb, Andrew. 2007. "To Play or not to Play: Making a Collection of Musical Instruments Accessible." In *The Power of Touch: Handling Objects in Museum and Heritage Contexts*, edited by Eliabeth Pye, 206–208. Walnut Creek, CA: Left Coast Press.

Vaughn, James M. 2008. "Rethinking the Rembrandt Rule." *Museum News* 87(2): 33–35, 71.

9

#MEANING

Cataloging Active Collections

Paul Bourcier

The Wisconsin Historical Society's collections include a fiberglass trade figure of a rotund lad dressed in red-and-white-checkered overalls hoisting a huge hamburger on a plate. From the standpoint of the curators who accepted the artifact, the object is both the product of Wisconsin manufacture (having been made by the FAST Corporation in Sparta in 1971) and an on-site tool for advertising and branding a Wisconsin restaurant (Marc's Big Boy in Madison) that was part of a national chain known for its signature double-decker ground beef sandwiches. As such, the object may be described and classified in a variety of useful ways that speak to local industry: the efficacy of fiberglass as a material for outdoor promotional mega fauna, the restaurant business, American dining habits, and even attitudes toward body image. But when the Historical Society occasionally places this artifact on display, it is most often met with nostalgic smiles. What meaning does the object hold for the beholder? What connections are made between trade figure and observer on both a visceral and intellectual level? What narratives do visitors bring to the experience? For those of us concerned with cataloging collections, can we effectively capture any of these myriad meanings?

Our systems of classifying museum collections have rarely tried to answer these questions. Instead they traditionally have been grounded in academic practice and have been designed to meet the needs of scholars and academically trained curators, archivists, and librarians. We seek to gain intellectual access to collections primarily by categorizing and indexing them in ways that are useful to researchers based on academic notions of what is important. We use terminology that describes the objects physically (the materials of which they are made, the techniques used to make them, their properties and attributes, their design elements), the functions they originally served, and the contexts of time, place, and people with which the objects are associated. These classifications of form, function, and association are certainly useful, but they do fairly little to bring us closer to explaining what these things actually mean to our audiences.

We know that once artifacts enter the museum, they assume new roles. The simple act of accepting grandmother's favorite mixing bowl changes it from something with a practical purpose to a display item. The original contexts of the artifacts no longer apply, but their meaning still remains changeable. In an article titled "The Cultural Biography of Objects," Chris Gosden and Yvonne Marshall discuss a concept called use life. They note that "as people and objects gather time, movement, and change, they are constantly transformed, and these transformations of person and object are tied up with each other" (1999, 169). This idea of changeable meaning over time creates complications for cataloging systems. Most history museums base their cataloging on an artifact's original function. This system, pioneered in the 1970s by Robert Chenhall and his colleagues, provided the museum profession with its first widely used, standardized vocabulary for naming objects and classifying them into ten categories defined by original function. Chenhall determined that all furnishings, transportation artifacts, and recreational objects should be primarily viewed by their function when they were made—even if this function changed during the artifact's time of use. If you instead allow that museum artifacts have a changeable "use life," the schema of Chenhall's *Nomenclature for Museum Cataloging* becomes useless as all objects, no matter the purpose for which they were created, would belong in Chenhall's "Category 8: Communication Objects" as soon as they entered a museum's collection.

Clearly, our current cataloging systems do not allow this type of flexibility. However, if our mission is to ensure that museums have "active collections," we must find a way to classify objects based on the "actions" they now assume or have the potential to assume for visitors. Objects in museum collections are cultural resources that serve both a variety of purposes and a variety of audiences, and our cataloging should acknowledge this fact.

I believe objects are transformed not only when they become part of a museum's collections, but again when the museum's audiences encounter them. Meaning is determined not by the original makers and users of the objects, nor by the museums that hold them, but by museum audiences. Thus the true power of making meaning from museum collections rests not with staff, but with visitors. The perspectives of museum staff are likely broadly different from those of museum users who may find meaning in collections in a number of different ways.

In this chapter I offer three concepts for discussion regarding the description and classification of collections and how new practices may get us closer to cataloging meaning-making:

1. Considering the roles that collections play in fulfilling our museums' missions and meeting audience needs.
2. Adding new ways to describe objects that go beyond intellectual access and explore the collections' impact on emotion and behavior.
3. Sharing the task of describing and classifying collections with the audiences who provide meaning.

Fulfilling the Mission

Despite their limitations, the ways we classify and catalog collections provide a standardized language and order that are useful to researchers. One cataloging tool, Library of Congress Subject Headings (LCSH), has long been a standard for hierarchically classifying the topics associated with cultural resources, but the fact that LCSH organizes terms into broad branches of knowledge (e.g., science, economics) betrays an academic bias that doesn't necessarily serve museum audiences who don't think or interact with collections the way researchers do (Library of Congress Subject Headings, 2016). In a profession in which curators are increasingly sharing authority and museums are seeking civic engagement, the idea of "active collections" needs to be described in terms that more effectively address the value they have for audiences.

If our collections are meant to educate, we might classify them in terms that address the curriculum standards of teachers in the arts, humanities, and sciences. If teachers were to describe our collections in terms that are valuable to them, what terms would they use? They might see the objects in terms of the functions the artifact originally served, or they might see objects as tools for helping students understand such educational goals as civic and environmental responsibility, cultural understanding, or making informed economic choices. Other audiences, such as those who derive creative inspiration from museum collections, might find other useful descriptions. Collectors and hobbyists need different types of information and how museums classify the collections could serve to delight this audience and increase their use or interest.

There are those who have personal associations with the objects we curate, not just donors and their descendants, but other people for whom our collections trigger personal memories based on any number of details related to memory and identity. How do we classify objects by their ability to evoke this feeling of connection? I once heard former Missouri Historical Society president Robert Archibald (2000) say that in our new paradigm, museums do not impose a narrative on the public but rather help the public construct a meaningful narrative. If we want to classify collections by the meanings they have, we need to recognize that collections are potential resources for transformative audience experiences. They inspire, stir emotions, stimulate ideas, evoke awe and wonder, and make other people's experiences real and tangible. I was reminded of this when reading a review by Chicago Tribune reporter Steve Johnson of the Chicago History Museum's exhibit, "The Secret Lives of Objects." Johnson wrote that the exhibit is a "testament to the power an object can hold":

> It is difficult to be in the presence of the lamp that started the 1903 Iroquois Theatre fire, presented alongside the door hardware there that prevented 600 people from exiting to safety, without thinking about those poor souls that wanted only an afternoon's entertainment.
>
> It is inspiring to see the letters from the sign at Palm Tavern, the famous Bronzeville jazz club, and imagine the greats who passed under those letters.
>
> (Johnson, 2015)

Going beyond the Intellectual

Gerhardus Robert Stewart discussed a new paradigm about connecting society and individuals and framed the issue within the three divisions of modern psychology: cognitive (concerning mental processes), affective (dealing with emotional processes), and conative (dealing with actions based on thoughts and feelings) (Stewart, 2014). Again, our profession is pretty good at classifying collections as sources of knowledge, although our systems for classifying that knowledge may not be useful for non-academic audiences.

"Active collections" can also derive their meaning from the feelings they evoke. In 2011, the National Museum of American History displayed objects from the 9/11 terrorist attacks such as the flight crew log from United Airlines Flight 93, a stairwell sign from the World Trade Center, and a door from a Brooklyn fire truck. Associate Director for Curatorial Affairs David Allison noted in a blog post:

> Our display will be a museum experience reduced to its essence: we will show artifacts that the Smithsonian has chosen to preserve in perpetuity to document this turning point in our history. As we view and contemplate them, they give us continued insight about what happened and why, and how events of that day are affecting our present and future. It is a relationship that matures over time. While these artifacts stay the same, we move on. Their meaning continually changes.
>
> Some day in the future, the museum's role will be to provide extensive commentary on these objects, to restore our memory of the events, and put them into broad historical context. How many planes were there again? What sites did they hit? What made the towers collapse?
>
> But not yet. Not this year. Our goal on this tenth anniversary is to stimulate personal memories. These objects ask each viewer to look back at the shock and horror of that day, and answer the simple question: How has this historic event changed your life?
>
> *(Allison, 2011)*

The Smithsonian recognized the affective value as well as the cognitive value of these objects. Classifying these objects functionally as a flight log, a sign, and a door doesn't even begin to address what these artifacts mean. We can try to move beyond the object's original function to add context, but simply assigning a subject heading such as "terrorism" to these objects still does not do anything to address the emotional impact of these objects on the museum's audiences.

If we can attempt to classify museum collections by the emotions they stir in those who encounter them, we may get closer to finding relevance and value for the visitor. If we classify museum collections by the emotions they stir in those who encounter them, however, we also need to decide who is best equipped to make these classifications. If so, a clear and transparent choice needs to be made— either authority rests with curators, or it rests with those audiences who experience these emotions.

Sharing the Task of Description

Even more challenging is considering how to catalog museum collections based on their *potential* to impact behavior. The History Relevance Campaign (a group of professionals seeking to promulgate the value of history) asserts that, "our connections and commitment to one another are strengthened when we share stories and experiences" (History Relevance Campaign, 2014). They argue that history (and by extension history museum collections) has the power to foster engaged citizens and inspire leadership, and these results are manifest through a change in behavior. In her book, *The Participatory Museum*, Nina Simon, drawing on the work of sociologist and engineer Jyri Engeström, writes about "social objects"—those museum artifacts that spark conversation. Examples she gives include an old stove that causes museum visitors to share memories of their grandmother's kitchen and an unsettling historical image people feel compelled to discuss (see Simon, 2010, Chapter 4).

I think most museum professionals would agree that objects that stimulate social interaction among visitors are valuable, but how can we classify artifacts that have this potential? Simon divides "social objects" into four categories and these classifications could provide a framework for describing objects in museum collections that provoke discussion:

- **Active**. Objects in motion. Ones whose operations produce an experience for visitors to share. Objects used in demonstrations definitely fall into this category.
- **Provocative**. Objects that stimulate discussion because they are simply surprising to visitors who encounter them. A giant ball of yarn provokes surprise and raises immediate questions about why someone would make it.
- **Relational**. Objects that invite interpersonal use. These pieces demand engagement by multiple people to function or be fully understood. Think of an assembly line or a tandem bike.
- **Personal**. Things with which museum visitors have a personal connection. This is simultaneously both an easy and a challenging category as "one of the challenges for cultural professionals is remembering that visitors don't come to the door with the same emotional investment and history with artifacts that professionals have and may not see them as obvious conversation pieces" (Simon, 2010, Chapter 4).

Despite the challenges, thinking of collections based on their potential to make the world a better place could be well worth the effort. To borrow again from the History Relevance Campaign, collections can provide tangible connections to stories that teach lessons about past challenges, decisions, and multiple perspectives, and help inform discussions about effective solutions for contemporary issues (History Relevance Campaign, 2014). Staff at the Wisconsin Historical Society witnessed this recently when one of the Society's board members brought in a group of juvenile offenders to see the collection of Daisy Bates.

As head of the Arkansas NAACP, Daisy Bates was instrumental in coordinating and mentoring the "Little Rock Nine," the first black students integrated into Arkansas public schools in 1957. As a result of her leadership in the Civil Rights Movement, she became a target of the Ku Klux Klan. In 1957 a baseball-sized rock shattered the front window of Daisy Bates' home with a note attached that read, "The next will be dynamite. KKK." The rock and note are in the national civil rights collection of the Wisconsin Historical Society (WHS). After a 16-year-old Community Option for Re-Engagement (CORE) Academy participant toured the WHS Archives, the WHS reported that the young man was moved beyond words when he saw the object.

> Holding the Daisy Bates rock in his hands, [he] connected with the American civil rights movement in an entirely new, strikingly personal way. Through the power of this object, a teenager was given a glimpse of life beyond himself and fundamentally changed the way he sees the world.
>
> *(Wisconsin Historical Society, 2016)*

Isn't this what we hope that museums and their collections can do for our visitors—to change how they see the world? The story of this simple rock shows how an artifact can be active in a meaningful way. We're certainly able to index this piece with a subject term such as "Civil Rights" but that hardly seems sufficient to describe the meaning this item had for that teenager. More importantly, is there a way to give the teenager a way to express what the rock means to him? Clearly museums do not have the only authoritative voice in contextualizing objects.

The Philadelphia History Museum mounted an exhibition called "The Ordinary, the Extraordinary, and the Unknown: The Power of Objects." The exhibit's creators noted that "on their own, objects may seem to have little meaning. It is the stories, emotions, and the connections we bring to them that give them life—and power" (Philadelphia History Museum, 2016). Our conventional means of classifying collections provide us intellectual access to the stories, but we need to find more worthwhile ways to describe and categorize objects by emotions and connections—the key qualities that are critical to meaning-making. Focusing only on describing the morphology of objects and their original function and context, centered around makers and users, has unintentionally limited our ability to connect our collections with audiences and helped ensure museum workers are the ones who still hold the power in defining the relationship between artifacts and visitors.

We know, however, that despite our efforts at interpretation, ultimately meaning is defined by our audiences. What if we explicitly acknowledged this and released control to visitors? The Portland Art Museum's "Object Stories" exhibit allows visitors to record their own personal perspectives on objects from the collection. As the museum's website explains, "Object Stories ruminates on the ways objects make us as fully as we make objects, and the myriad ways objects speak to and shape who we are—our ideas, emotions, values, relationships, and aesthetics" (Portland Art Museum, 2011). What if we took this idea and added audience perspectives to catalog records? We could then classify those stories in conjunction with the artifact record in order to create a catalog that focused on relationships and emotions.

Going one step further, what do we do to adopt a new model in which users themselves describe and classify collections in ways that serve their own needs? Some museums have already begun to explore this bottom-up concept of folk-sonomy. The Philadelphia Museum of Art (2016), for example, allows visitors to its website to add their own social tags to online collections. Social tagging reflects personal associations, categories, and concepts that are meaningful and relevant to the individual tagger.

Any museum that seeks to adopt an "active collections" model of collections management should first consider how meaning is made. Traditional methods of contextualizing and classifying museum objects play a role in fostering intellectual access and understanding, but they provide only a catalyst for meaning-making. The rest comes from the thoughts, feelings, and actions of museum audiences who encounter museum collections and the stories they document, illustrate, and make tangible. It will require a reexamination of our assumptions about our audiences and sharing the authority of our collection catalogs, but new classification systems could potentially substantially deepen our users' interaction with museum collections.

References

Allison, David K. 2011. "September 11: Experience the Power of Objects First-Hand." National Museum of American History blog, August 9. http://americanhistory.si.edu/blog/2011/08/september-11-experience-the-power-of-objects-first-hand.html.

Archibald, Robert. 2000. Lecture presented to the Wisconsin Historical Society, Madison, WI, May 1.

Chenhall, Robert G. 1978. *Nomenclature for Museum Cataloging: A System for Classifying Man-Made Objects*. Nashville, TN: American Association for State and Local History. Most recently revised in 2015 as *Nomenclature 4.0 for Museum Cataloging*.

Gosden, Chris, and Yvonne Marshall. 1999. "The Cultural Biography of Objects." *World Archaeology* 31: 169–178.

History Relevance Campaign. 2014. *Value Statement*. https://www.historyrelevance.com/value-statement.

Johnson, Steve. 2015. "'The Secret Lives of Objects' Exhibit at the Chicago History Museum." *Chicago Tribune*, March 25. http://www.chicagotribune.com/entertainment/museums/ct-secret-lives-of-objects-20150325-column.html.

Library of Congress. "Subject Headings." http://id.loc.gov/authorities/subjects.

Philadelphia History Museum. 2012. http://www.philadelphiahistory.org/exhibition/power-of-objects/

Philadelphia Museum of Art. 2016. http://www.philamuseum.org/collections/socialTagging.html.

Portland Art Museum. 2011. http://www.objectstories.org/about/index.html

Simon, Nina. 2010. *The Participatory Museum*. Santa Cruz, CA: Museum 2.0.

Stewart, Gerhardus Robert. 2014. "The Impact of Film and Television on the Individual and Society." B.A. dissertation, Middlesex University.

Wisconsin Historical Society. 2015. *Columns* 36(4): 3.

QUESTION THE DATABASE!

Vickie Stone

At the 2016 American Alliance of Museums' Annual Meeting, I had the pleasure to moderate a panel titled "The Culturally Responsive Database," which explored much of the content below. I am thankful to the panelists Terri Anderson and Emily Houf, both catalogers for the Smithsonian's National Museum of African American History and Culture, for sharing the excellent work that their department and institution is doing in striving for a more culturally responsive database.

When striving to create active collections, it can be easy to get stuck on the materiality of the objects we are talking about. Where will they be stored? In which exhibits will the objects be used? How can the objects be used for tactile programs? Yet, much of the information needed to make decisions about how an object can be effectively used are found outside of its physical nature and proposed use. Museums are brokers and facilitators of historical content, scientific knowledge, cultural traditions, and increasingly moral and emotional types of information. These less tangible ways of understanding are also embodied in museum objects, but that information may be obscured if our cataloging focuses exclusively on materiality. Today, non-physical information is often found only informally as part of the institutional memory instead of inside the museum's formal recordkeeping system, the database.

Database systems are the integral core of maintaining museum information. They are used to order, categorize, and ultimately control intellectual and physical aspects of objects. These systems document both the tangible (storage location, condition, use, etc.) and intangible (an object's "story," history, meaning, etc.) properties of objects. Without these database systems we may not be able to answer some of the basic questions about how to make collections active, such as "how many objects do we have like this one?" or "does this object have a compelling history?"

It is clear that not only do collection *objects* need to become active, but also object *information*. I believe we can modify database systems to activate them to their full potential. New models of active collections management demand new models of active database management.

One of those models may be to create database systems that are more "culturally responsive." I describe cultural responsiveness as the incorporation of multiple, decentralized perspectives that both challenge and enrich a fluid cataloging practice. There is no standard model for a culturally responsive database, as every institution has both unique collections and constituencies. However, there are four aspects of database management that I feel should be incorporated into a database in order to more fully make collections databases active and culturally responsive.

Language

If an art museum's collection comprises paintings that depict historical medical procedures and photographs of microscopic biology, then an art cataloging standard such as the J. Paul Getty Museum's (n.d.) *Art & Architecture Thesaurus* may only be appropriate in categorizing a portion of the objects' essence. The inclusion of medical or scientific terminology would be necessary in order to have comprehensive metadata about the collection. A key aspect of any database is considering what taxonomies and lexicon systems will be adopted or adapted. How might your institution's database privilege one group over another in its use of a standardized language? Should your institution standardize categories or deviate from preexisting lists? Who makes those decisions? Language also includes thinking about the integration of bilingual or multilingual systems. Does the database privilege the English term over the original artist's, source community's, or scientific language? How may a multilingual system improve or complicate searches?

Identities and Communities

Identities such as race, gender, sexuality, age, and others are all significant pieces of information to have recorded in relation to an object's history. For the art museum previously mentioned, not only could the identities of artists be explored, but also the identities of people depicted or relevant communities (following appropriate laws such as HIPPA for patient identification, as appropriate). Beyond individual identities, being sensitive and cognizant of how scientific and medical practice has been shaped by cultural influences and how those have affected individual communities would be important to include into specific object information. How might addressing identities in a database either silence or promote specific communities or people? How might cataloging practices contribute to a more intersectional, inclusive perspective of collections?

Access and Authority Levels

At the hypothetical art museum, whose collection is partially available online, there are a series of photographs of indigenous medical practice that are deemed sacred.

Some community members have identified that the public viewing of those photos is inappropriate, and the museum should consider working with the community and elders to restrict viewing access for those catalog entries. Questions to consider in relation to database access and authority levels are: Who is using your institution's database system and why? Is the database only for internal use by curators and collections managers? Is the database used by researchers or is it the basis of public access online? Who is able to input information? We have traditionally used systems designed by museum professionals for their own use. However, there is incredible potential for stakeholders outside of the museum institution to contribute to museum information capacity building through tagging schemes, authority to enter specific fields of entry, or by adding emotional comment/multimedia responses.

Functionality

Setting up and recording all of that information in a database would be useless if there was no easy way to extract it. If a researcher was looking at the art museum for works that depict plague doctors, they might return different entries if they search for a term such as "beak" instead of "doctor's mask." Even if both terms are in the catalog entry, the field of entry that each term was entered into would determine how the returned list would be prioritized. Searchability and report generation are key components to database systems. Knowing who is using the database and what types of information those constituencies are looking for will help address how they want to search for it.

The potential for active and culturally responsive database systems to contribute to better collections management, and even in justifying museum relevancy, is tremendous. What if a museum's data actually reflected the cultural diversity of its collection? What if that data was not only generated internally by staff, but by community members? Would we be better equipped to make good accession and hard deaccessioning decisions because we would be informed by a multitude of perspectives?

Certainly obtaining this type of information and changing the way that databases are managed seems daunting and labor intensive. Database systems are expensive to maintain no matter what the content may be. Striving to make them more inclusive would maximize the investment of populating and sustaining them by making collections information more useful both internally and externally to the institution. Culturally responsive databases that are active in addressing these questions would lead to a refined mission-driven practice.

Reference

J. Paul Getty Museum. n.d. *Art & Architecture Thesaurus Online.* http://www.getty.edu/research/tools/vocabularies/aat/index.html.

10

PRACTICAL STRATEGIES FOR ADDRESSING HOARDING IN COLLECTIONS

Gail Steketee

This chapter is an adaptation of several psychological treatment methods described by Tolin et al. (2014) in a self-help guide for people seeking to reduce their serious hoarding problems. It attempts to apply these intervention strategies to a museum collections context in order to provide the museum field with some new tools for dealing with overgrown collections. The intervention strategies derive from individual, group, and educational workshops aimed at improving hoarding from a cognitive (thoughts, beliefs) and behavioral (action) perspective. A first question to ask is whether there is a problem with excessive acquisitions and/or the need to deaccession. Motivation to address these issues will partly depend on how the problem is defined, and whether it is considered important enough to warrant serious attention by the leaders and staff of the organization. Suggested interventions focus on modifying unhelpful beliefs that interfere with making progress on deaccessioning, as well as improving organizational systems and problem-solving skills.

Is There a Problem?

An important first question is whether museum leaders and staff believe there is a collections problem that warrants some sort of intervention. That is, is the museum's mission being impaired by too much stuff in the collections that is not well-organized? Are the exhibitions, programming, and outreach efforts accomplishing the museum's goals for the public? If not, is part of the problem that the sheer volume of material that staff find too large to manage is distracting the institution from other important, mission-driven work?

If the answers to these questions are generally "Yes," a first step is to consider the museum's basic values and its goals for the foreseeable future. Unless these values and goals are kept front and center, it will be difficult to maintain motivation to proceed with next steps. Strategic planning is often an avenue for reminding everyone of those values and goals, and identifying potential barriers to accomplishing them. These very first questions to ask should be routine practice in museums, but if they have not been answered, this is the first step!

- What basic values underlie our mission?
- What are the long-term goals for the overall collection and new acquisitions?
- Do our goals fit our values and mission and do they serve our stakeholders well?
- Are the goals realistic for the budget and staffing needed to manage the collection?
- Are the current acquisition and deaccessioning strategies working well to meet the long-term goals?

Answers to these questions will help the leadership decide whether to act, and will help keep everyone's eyes on the prize. Threats to motivation to work on obvious problems can derive from leadership and staff. Some may report simple lack of awareness ("We've always done it this way. I had no idea that anyone was unhappy"), denial despite contradictory evidence ("They always complain, but our collections and procedures are just fine. There's no problem here"), and mistaken assumptions that solutions may be found just around the corner with a little more effort ("We just need to work harder and get one more collections grant and it will all be resolved in a few months"). One method for clarifying whether there is in fact a problem is to ask all employees and knowledgeable observers to rate the extent of the problem(s) with acquisition, management, and retention of objects, and the extent to which the current collection supports mission, values, and audience. Significant discrepancies in reporting probably signal a problem and a lack of insight and therefore motivation on some people's part.

Misleading Assumptions, Mistaken Beliefs, and Emotional Reactions

How people think about objects can be a major source of trouble for making progress on managing those objects. Psychiatrist Aaron T. Beck and others have demonstrated that behavior is determined by a person's thoughts and the resulting feelings those thoughts provoke, which lead to actions (Beck 1976). Thus, the assumptions people make about their possessions is an important trigger for their acquiring and saving behavior. This is especially evident when an emotional reaction seems exaggerated or out of place. Whenever that happens, it is especially helpful to ask oneself, "What's going through my mind right now?" Below are some common hoarding belief "traps" that may be especially relevant to the management of museum collections with the language adapted to the museum context.

Potential Usefulness

A common reason for keeping objects is that they are "useful." In many cases, the person believes they have the *potential* to be useful even if they are not useful now. The thought goes,

- "This could undergo full conservation treatment one day when there is time and funding."
- "It's a shame not to keep this. We might want to use it in an exhibition about X one day."
- "It would be wasteful to let this go."

But in fact, such objects often require considerable time, energy, and money to make them *actually* useful. The important question is whether that time, effort, and money will truly help to achieve the organization's goals (would an exhibition about X actually serve the museum's mission and audience in a meaningful way, for example).

Perfectionism and Fear of Making Mistakes

People who hoard often worry about making a bad choice: "What if I accidentally throw away something important? That would be awful." Small mistakes are labeled a "failure," producing feelings of inadequacy and helplessness and interfering with efforts to move forward. Perfectionism stems from common mistakes in thinking, such as "all-or-nothing thinking" in black and white terms without considering the shades of gray. Some examples are:

- "We need to find the perfect place to put this, and fully catalog it too; just leave it here for now."
- "We can't get rid of this until we have reviewed it thoroughly and considered all possible angles."

But is that really true? The old saying goes: "You can't make an omelet without breaking some eggs." Mistakes happen—even when you are holding collections in the public trust. It is inevitable that at some point valuable items will be removed, misplaced, and damaged; a zero-loss mindset is not realistic. The top priority is to meet the organization's most important goals, even if some mistakes occur along the way.

Responsibility and Guilt

Many people feel guilty when they consider downsizing their stuff or not acquiring something offered to them, as if they were being irresponsible or wasteful. Some feel compelled to make sure that the unwanted objects go to a "good home," someplace that will use them or deserves to have them. These beliefs often have "should" and "ought" statements in them:

- "This is in good condition, so we should find the right place for it."
- "It's a shame to let this go. Maybe we ought to take it."

Emotional Attachment and Loss

Emotional attachment is a powerful motivator that leads many people to keep items that have little practical use or aesthetic value. When people often attach emotions to objects, the problem is magnified. Beliefs might be:

- "We got that as a gift from X. How could we let that go?"
- "This reminds me so much of our early days. We could find a use for it."

Control

Some people keep items simply to exercise control over that area of their lives. The more other people complain about it and urge getting rid of things, the more they want to keep them. The belief is:

- "I am in control here. No one has the right to tell me what to do with this [my] stuff."

While it is true that people who own objects have the right to do with them as they please, the downside is that digging in one's heels leads to more entrenched beliefs and problems with the objects themselves.

Overthinking

Variants of overthinking include being a bit too creative about the uses of objects and setting burdensome rules for getting rid of them. Some people tend to think of many different ways to use objects that represent a myriad of wonderful opportunities:

- "Just imagine what we could do with this!"

Technically, it is true that a wooden box can serve many functions—holding items, a step to reach something high, and many other things. But such creative ideas can also prevent people from parting with items they have no intention of using anytime soon, so the objects simply contribute to clutter and confusion.

People may also set complicated and burdensome rules for parting with objects, such as bundling newspapers carefully so the recycling crew is not critical of sloppy bundles at the curb. Such exacting "rules" become such a major ordeal that almost nothing is discarded. The belief goes something like this:

- "These items can only be discarded if . . ."

Evaluating and Changing Beliefs

The following questions, adapted from treatment for people who hoard, may prove helpful in examining beliefs about the value of and need for current objects or potential acquisitions:

1. How many of these do we already have? Is that enough to meet our goals?
2. Do we have enough time to actually make it useful?
3. Has anyone used this in the past year?
4. Do we have a specific plan to use this within a reasonable timeframe?
5. Does this fit our mission and our current goals?
6. How does this compare with other objects we already have? Is the quality, accuracy, or value high enough to meet our needs?
7. Does this seem important just because I'm looking at it now?
8. If we didn't already own this, would we acquire it now?
9. Do we really need it?
10. Could we acquire it again if we found we really needed it?
11. Do we have enough space to display or store this without expanding our current footprint?
12. Realistically, what will happen if we don't follow these "rules"? What happens?

Another strategy for evaluating an object is to consider the *advantages and disadvantages* of keeping or acquiring it versus letting it go. Sometimes writing these down on paper helps tip the scale in favor of letting go.

Another evaluative strategy is to investigate *need versus want*. Does the organization really *need* the item or do the decision-makers just *want* it? Need presumes a definite fit with organizational mission and value so that not having it would be clearly problematic. Want, on the other hand, means a desire, a preference (in a perfect world, all things being equal), and most likely that keeping it would make the evaluator feel better than letting it go, but in fact, the organization will be OK without it. Need and want can each be rated on 10-point scales from 1 (not at all) to 10 (very much), and if want outweighs need, the decision is clearer.

Finally, behavioral experiments can help test whether the value of the item is as strong as it seems. This begins with a specific prediction of (1) what bad outcome would occur if the item in question was no longer available, and (2) how difficult it would be to manage if the bad outcome happened. Then, put the item someplace else that is inaccessible for a little while (e.g., ask someone else on staff to put it in an undisclosed section of collections storage or otherwise segregate it from the rest of the collection, closed off and removed from view) in order to act *as if* it is no longer available. After a useful period of time (a week, a few weeks), come back to the original predictions: Did the bad outcome actually occur? If the bad outcome did happen, does it still seem as difficult to recover as predicted?

These strategies of asking questions, evaluating advantages/disadvantages, rating need versus want, and behavioral experiments to test predictions may be potential methods for identifying, examining, and managing beliefs about objects that get in the way of healthy collections stewardship.

Getting Organized

Developing and keeping an organizational system for objects is an ongoing challenge. Most individuals organize their possessions by categories: linens go in the linen closet, canned and dry food belong in cupboards or the pantry, tax returns live in a file cabinet, etc. But people who hoard tend to rely on visual cues, generally using piles so objects sit out where they can see them.

Unfortunately, that strategy often leads to a mixture of important and unimportant things being piled together because no one sorts and puts things away on a regular basis. Too many objects and limited storage space complicate the problem. The museum already has best practices in place for identifying and selecting categories, and for systematically filing and storing items consistent with institutional needs. The issue is whether the ongoing maintenance of these organization systems can be achieved with existing staffing and funding. If not, it is probably more realistic to reconsider the current size and scope of the collection than to expect additional resources will address the problem.

Problem-Solving Strategies

It is inevitable that the best-laid plans will go awry at some point, necessitating the use of problem solving skills within the organization. Confidence in these skills will help prevent becoming frustrated, overwhelmed, and derailed by unexpected challenges that arise. The following simple steps are recommended:

1. Identify and define the problem—the trick here is to be as clear and specific as possible. What exactly is the problem people are facing that is getting in the way of healthy collections stewardship?
2. Generate as many solutions as possible—the goal is to brainstorm lots of ideas, even silly ones, without yet evaluating them critically. Keep the thinking flexible and creative, without dumping on anyone's ideas. Running off to Timbuktu might be among them.
3. Evaluate the possible solutions—does the idea make sense? Is it feasible?
4. Select one or two ideas that seem most practical and implement one—actually try it to see what happens.
5. Evaluate the outcome—was it helpful, neutral, or harmful?
6. If it didn't solve the problem adequately, try the second strategy and see if that improves the situation. Start over again if neither idea works well.

Summary and Comment

These suggestions derive from treating individuals with serious hoarding problems. Whether they will prove helpful for organizations such as museums that also appear to have similar problems with excessive acquisitions and difficulty downsizing when needed is not known. For those who are interested in reading more about hoarding disorder and its treatment, information and reference materials are available at the International OCD Foundation, as well as through a number of other web-based resources such as Oxford University Press, which has published several books on the treatment of hoarding from a self-help, individual and group treatment perspective, and community-based strategies for severe involuntary cases (see www.iocdf.org/hoarding; https://global.oup.com/academic/search?q=hoarding&cc=us&lang=en).

References

Beck, Aaron T. 1979. *Cognitive Therapy and the Emotional Disorders*. New York: Meridian Press.

Tolin, David F., Randy O. Frost, and Gail Steketee. 2014. *Buried in Treasures: Help for Compulsive Acquiring, Saving, and Hoarding*. 2nd edition. New York: Oxford University Press.

TIDYING UP MUSEUM COLLECTIONS

Anne Jordan

In her bestselling book *The Life-Changing Magic of Tidying Up*, Marie Kondo (2014) writes about the most important things to remember while discarding and organizing an individual's belongings. This book was written for personal use and is geared toward average people at home, but many of her points can be adapted for a museum's collection. Listed below are seven points adapted from Kondo's work to remember while working in the collection room.

1. The Collection Does Not Need to Be the Biggest in the Land

The norm in museum culture has been to highlight and brag about the size of a collection—but if the public cannot access 90% of these objects, why does it matter that a museum cares for thousands of artifacts? Kondo states, "The fact that you possess a surplus of things that you can't bring yourself to discard doesn't mean you are taking good care of them. In fact, it is quite the opposite" (126). Having a smaller collection could be just as desirable; each object could get better, more specialized, care and attention.

2. Do Not Simply Rearrange the Collection

"Putting things away creates the illusion that the clutter problem has been solved" (23). Just because objects are hidden in boxes does not mean that a collection is clean and organized. The problem still exists; it is just no longer visible. Instead of focusing only on organization, try deaccessioning less desirable items. It might cure some of the anxiety created from the complications of caring for large, ever-growing collections.

3. Is the Object Ever Used/Displayed? If Not, Get Rid of It!

Objects in a collection should be exciting and useful. If they are not used and are only collecting dust, who is benefiting from keeping them around? One of the most useful exercises Kondo writes about is to "take each item in one's hand and ask: 'Does this spark joy?' If it does, keep it. If not, dispose of it" (41). This process helps demonstrate what items fit the mission, the goals, or the museum's purpose, and which ones are only placeholders. "We should be choosing what we want to keep, not what we want to get rid of" (41). If the focus is only on the negative aspect of tidying up, the process feels daunting and depressing. Instead, keep the process positive and remember everything has a home; it may just be at another institution.

4. Do Not Add Artifacts Simply Because One Is Not in the Collection. Similarly, Do Not Keep Artifacts Simply Because They Have Always Been There

Many museum professionals claim that they cannot get rid of items because they may need them in the future. According to Kondo (45),

> People have trouble discarding things that they could still use (functional value), that contain helpful information (informational value), and that have sentimental ties (emotional value). When these things are hard to obtain or replace (rarity), they become even harder to part with.

How realistic is it to keep certain items based on a future belief? Some artifacts may never be useful for an institution, so why keep them around? Always keep in mind the museum's mission and goal when determining the value or use of an object.

5. Do Not Have "Parents" in the Room while Discarding

During deaccessioning, donors can become overly sensitive and attached to their donated objects. If this becomes problematic, it may help to imagine donors as the object's parents who insist "you can't get rid of that." This exercise will give museum professionals a better perspective for dealing with donors. In line with Kondo's teachings, donors should be alerted that the discarding process is taking place, but not allowed to see their objects being taken away nor allowed to dictate what stays and what goes without regard to policy: "Parents can find it very painful to see clothes, toys, and mementos from the past on the rubbish heap" (48). Make it clear the museum is not throwing away the artifacts; it is finding them a new home. Since the donors gave the museum the item they will (hopefully) understand the museum has a right to part with it. Again, be upfront with them through the whole process. Transparency will help everyone transition through the change.

6. Let the Objects Know They Were Loved

When it is time to part with objects the museum no longer needs, celebrate the object's life with staff and visitors. Make it an occasion where everyone can see the importance of the object before it goes. "Send it off joyfully with words like, 'Thank you for finding me,' or 'Have a good journey. See you soon!'" (193). The museum staff, board, and donors will appreciate the care taken in the discarding process.

7. Do Not Fear the Future . . . Embrace It!

In the beginning deaccessioning will be hard, but don't fret; everything will be all right. "One of the magical effects of tidying is confidence in your decision-making capacity" (178). Throughout the process, museum workers will get a better feel of what the museum needs and, more importantly, what it does not need. "You will come to a point where you suddenly know how much is just right for you" and will be able to say "no thank you" to objects that do not fit the museum's mission and the collection will flourish because of it (124).

Reference

Kondo, Marie. 2014. *The Life-Changing Magic of Tidying Up: The Japanese Art of Decluttering and Organizing*. Berkeley, CA: Ten Speed Press.

11

THINGS IN FLUX

Collecting in the Constructivist Museum

Benjamin Filene

Perhaps nowhere is there a greater gulf between what museums actually do and what the public *thinks* we do than in the realm of collecting. Our audiences don't see acquiring objects as an interpretive act, one that involves prioritizing one thing over another; and they don't realize that we choose things to advance a particular vision of history or science or art. Visitors tend to believe that we collect objectively, eternally.

Mostly we have ourselves to blame. Museum professionals have not managed to convey to our audiences what we are really up to in building collections. That's not surprising since we have largely failed to confront the truth ourselves. In policy and practice, most museums still collect in ways that presume objective curators who can make sense of the whole world for all time. Really, though, we know that we are not objective and omniscient. We recognize that knowledge is shifting and contingent, that today's grand vision will look so early twenty-first-century to the next generation. How can we do justice to the slipperiness of knowledge in the all-so-tangible world of objects? How can we build collections that show we are in the interpretation business, that convey to visitors how museums *work*? In other words, how should museums collect for the constructivist world, where knowledge isn't gathered and held but made and remade?

Famously, Roy Rosenzweig and David Thelen in the mid-1990s found that visitors trusted museums more than any other source of information—more than professors, more than nonfiction books, more than grandma (Rosenzweig and Thelen 1998, 21–22). The museum field rejoiced, but behind the scenes many of us felt we had been given an undeserved gift: we knew the findings reflected a troubling misunderstanding of museum practice. Visitors trust museums, Rosenzweig and Thelen's survey showed, because they think museums present unmediated knowledge, that the objects on display are allowed to speak for themselves. That faith reflects a view of meaning-making in museums at odds with postmodern understandings of knowledge as a shifting, time-bound construct. As a learning theory stemming from the postmodernist insight, constructivism posits that knowledge is not eternal but is shaped through myriad decisions by content-producers and then filtered through the learner's own prisms of interest, attention, and prior understandings. The challenge for museums is to reconcile our collecting practices with our contemporary vision of knowledge.

Constructivist collecting need not involve a wholesale rejection of what came before, but it does demand greater self-awareness and transparency in the decisions we make about objects. We need to understand the legacies that constructivist collecting extends and departs from, so that we can be intentional about what kind of collecting we're doing when and why.

The Exceptional Collection

In the earliest museums, from the Renaissance into the nineteenth century, collecting was driven by a search for the exceptional. Cabinets of curiosity sought out the extreme and the singular—a purse made of spider's web, a horn that grew from an Englishwoman's forehead (Schwarzer 2012, 7–8). Implicitly, these collections showed the world to be strange and wonderful, full of wonder. Museums set out to dazzle and confound visitors with multiplicity. With its associations with Barnumesque freak shows, this sort of collecting is today often dismissed as unseemly or undisciplined, but the appeal of the exceptional survives and has its place: the biggest diamond, the first telephone, the oldest dinosaur bone.

Interest in the exceptional also underlay early museums' attraction to relics— ordinary objects that have acquired an aura by being associated with extraordinary people or events. Relic-seekers collected cut-out fragments of the original star-spangled banner and locks of George Washington's hair (Barnett 2013). Few museums today build their collection solely around these highly charged relics, but the impulse remains alive and well. A recent exhibition at the Chicago History Museum showcased not only Abe Lincoln's iconic top hat but also his family carriage and the bed on which he died. A guitar is just a guitar, but it becomes something very different if Jimi Hendrix played it.

The Completist Collection

Later in the nineteenth century, as the fields of science and then history professionalized, a new approach to knowledge—and to collecting—took hold. Instead of seeking the singular, professionals set out to gather and classify the typical—all of it. Museums sought to document the full extent of human knowledge and achievement through artifacts. This impulse to contain the world under glass drove some of the great collecting projects of the late nineteenth century—the Smithsonian (founded 1846), the American Museum of Natural History in New York (1876), the Metropolitan Museum of Art (1870). The challenge was vast, but implicit in the effort was the assumption that knowledge was finite: it could be tamed through hierarchy and system. As the complexity of knowledge proliferated, commitment to the completist project only increased: more sub-specialties, more elaborate classification systems, bigger storage areas.

Completism held sway for most of the twentieth century. Even seemingly revolutionary attacks on museum practice did not fundamentally upend the commitment to collecting the whole world. Proponents of the New Social History in the 1960s, for example, defiantly set out an alternative vision of who and what constituted America's past. Rejecting the elitism of a history driven by white men—the governors and generals of traditional textbooks—social historians aimed to rewrite history from the "bottom up," to include the experiences of, for instance, factory workers, farmers, women, and people of color.

Social history transformed how history museums in the late twentieth century saw their work as interpreters and collectors. Museums introduced a new cast of characters into their galleries, in path-breaking exhibitions such as the National Museum of American History's *Everyday Life in the American Past* (opened 1964), *A Nation of Nations* (1976), *After the Revolution: Everyday Life in America, 1780–1800* (1985), and *Field to Factory: Afro-American Migration, 1915–1940* (1989) (Post 2013, 45, 114). In these exhibitions, the objects that one might have seen in a traditional county history museum—the spinning wheel, the bonnet, the plow—took on new life and purpose as they were used to illustrate the experiences of people who had been marginalized from mainstream history.

As transformative as social history was, it did not reject certain core assumptions about museums and their missions. Social historians aimed to tell a broader and more inclusive American story, but they still assumed that there *was* an overarching story (Filene 2017). Curators attacked traditional collecting practices for under-representing women, minorities, and the working class, but they did not question the broader project of documenting the full range of life experience through objects: they challenged the incompleteness of the elites' collection, not their devotion to completism.

The Constructivist Collection

In a history museum, the completist collection takes a Noah's Ark attitude, gathering a representative one or two of everything. The underlying assumption is that the museum will leave a full account of the past to the future. In some respects, it's an admirable approach, one still very much with us today. Indeed, with heightened attention to inclusivity over the last several decades, museums are collecting more than ever before, representing a wider swath of human experience. As essays in this volume document, however, the completist impulse can overwhelm even the largest museum's resources (see Tisdale, this volume).

As pressing as the resource problem is, even more urgent is an intellectual dilemma: our completism is inherently incomplete. The issue is not the size of our storage facilities but the fact that knowledge itself refuses to be pinned down. As Nick Merriman, director of the Manchester Museum, suggests, we need to "challeng[e] the notion that museums still function as repositories of objects and specimens that represent an objective record of collective memory." Collections, he writes, "should be seen for what they are: partial, historically contingent assemblages that reflect the tastes and interests of both the times and the individuals who made them" (Merriman 2008, 3). We aren't collecting once and for all but in the here and now.

Addressing this intellectual challenge is the way to tackle the resource problem. If we can envision a vibrant approach to constructivist collecting, we can move past completism, not with a feeling of resignation and inadequacy but with a sense of purpose. So what would constructivist collecting look like? Stepping away from the myth of our objectivity has implications for what we collect and how. Here are four categories of objects the constructivist curator might pursue.

Storytelling Objects

The constructivist collection seeks objects that convey interpretations and that have the potential to communicate to our publics how interpretation works. One way to approach constructivist collecting comes directly out of the social history impulse. Fundamentally, social history curators wanted to use objects to tell stories of ordinary people. If we consider story-driven collecting through the constructivist instead of completist lens, we can see one route to a more contingent kind of collecting. We can use social history tools for new purposes.

For instance, we can employ story-driven collecting to illustrate that there *is* no single story. A hat, for example, may generically illustrate a theme: factory-driven manufacturing techniques or transnational markets or 1920s fashion. Story-driven collecting seeks a more human dimension. The hat takes on a whole new meaning if a particular man in Mississippi put it on his head on a June morning in 1919 before heading to the train station to depart for a new life in Detroit. The object connects us to a person, and it enlivens and enriches our understanding of the journey he embarked on. The specificity of this story also invites recognition that an identical-looking hat could contain other stories. In other words, story-driven collecting makes clear that curators are in the choosing business. Looking for objects that help us tell stories gives us a rationale to pick one object over another. It's a way to explain to would-be artifact donors and to ourselves why we don't take a particular wedding dress or iron or toaster even if it's old or pretty or, even, rare: we're not looking just for things but for *stories*.

What kind of stories? This depends on the museum, its mission, and, honestly, on the predilections of the curators. And we should also recognize that it depends on the moment in which we live. Take a nineteenth-century postcard that proudly shows belching smokestacks. Earlier generations might have collected it to represent industrial growth; in our age of climate change, though, we can see the image as a window into destructive assumptions about the environment. Similarly, a curator in 1947 might have collected a recording of "Zip-a-Dee-Doo-Dah" because it won an Academy Award that year for Best Original Song; in the time of Black Lives Matter, we see the song about carefree plantation life as telling a story about how twentieth-century mass media projected a sanitized vision of race relations in America.

Story-driven collecting is already common in many museums, often driven by the needs of particular exhibitions. Collections policies, though, tend to hang on to the completist illusion that we're dispassionately piecing together the past. The policies indicate what subjects and time periods we "cover" in our collections— "we document life in the Lowcountry region from 1700s to the present"—without distinguishing how or why. In their collecting policies, observes Simon J. Knell, museums "continue to conceive of objects as facts which can simply be gathered up. This belief rather overestimates the inherent qualities of the object and under- estimates the interpretive processes which make sense of the material world" (Knell 2004, 13–14).

Likewise, the ways we describe collecting to our constituencies invite confu- sion. We're collecting to "save the past for the future" or to "preserve history before it's too late." Certainly there is a forward-looking aspect to our work, but we should acknowledge openly that, in fact, we collect in the present and, to a great extent, *for* the present: we're *shaping* a legacy for the future. Our descendants will look at these objects and learn as much about us the collectors as about the times the objects represent.

Similarly, the language we use to describe artifacts obscures the interpretive nature of collecting. While most museums now resist the attic metaphor, the trope of "treasures" remains common. Treasure, though, suggests inherent worth, not instrumental use. As discussed above, certain relics (Abe Lincoln's hat, Dorothy's slippers) may warrant being celebrated for their singularity, but our audiences would better understand what we do if we ascribed value to our holdings not for their rarity and self-explanatory value but for the stories they enable us to tell. Things don't have innate meaning; museums are not treasure-keepers, but places where stories get made.

Invented Objects

If constructivist collecting often involves crafting stories around objects, it can also entail the opposite: literally constructing objects to represent a story. For an exhibi- tion at the Minnesota History Center (*Sounds Good to Me: Music in Minnesota*, open 2000–2007), we illustrated the behind-the-scenes workings of the music business by creating a fanciful ten-foot tower of objects depicting every item that Bob Dylan's 1986 performance contract required the Metrodome arena provide in his dressing room for him and his entourage. The contract listing the items was real; the teetering tower of bronzed M&M's, water bottles, and towels was just a visual representation, one clearly manufactured by the museum. In the constructivist museum, there is room for objects created ad hoc, including ones that are explicitly *not* designed to be preserved for posterity.

If the Dylan tower would traditionally be classified as a prop, the Smithsonian more literally created an artifact in April 2016 when it went to Lyles Station, Indiana, to gather dirt. In Washington, DC, the Indiana soil became an object, displayed at the new National Museum of African American History and Culture to represent the work of generations of African American farmers in the heartland, people underrepresented in collections that, historically, have privileged white culture. As the president of the Lyles Station Historical Corp. noted, until the Smithsonian's arrival, "No one's ever talked about" the region's African American farmers. "[T]he stories that were written down were the ones people wanted to hear" (McGlone 2016). Through its willful act of artifact-creation, the Smithsonian signaled its determination to overcome historical barriers and, as well, showed its hand as a shaper and interpreter of stories.

Multivalent Objects

Following from the emphasis on storytelling, another constructivist collecting technique is to look for objects that lend themselves to multiple points of view. One way to illustrate that meaning is not eternal is to show that the significance we find depends on through whose eyes we look. In this approach, "What is it?" becomes only the first and, likely, the least interesting information we seek about an object. Consider, for example, an ornate silver Victorian-era butter dish. After identifying the artifact's function, an obvious question would be "Who owned it?" But we can keep asking questions: Who made it? (a craftsman? a factory-worker?) Who sold it to whom? Was it advertised as a status symbol, a sign of wealth and attainment? How might it be perceived by the dinner guest who sat down and had no idea what it was or how to use it? Who polished the object, and how did that chore make them feel about it? Who saved it and, eventually, who decided to get rid of it, sending it on its way to the antique store (where I found it)? While we can't unearth such provenance and point of view for every artifact, we can bring additional focus to our collecting if we seek objects that offer rich answers to multivalent questions.

Calling attention to the multiple meanings attached to objects can also effectively illustrate to visitors the contingency of interpretation: different objects have different meanings in different contexts. That attention to multiplicity includes noting when a point of view is absent. Several of my exhibitions have focused on trying to unearth as many layers of stories as possible from a single object. In *Open House: If These Walls Could Talk* at the Minnesota History Center (2006–present), we worked to discover the stories of the residents over time who lived in a single ordinary house—fifty families across 125 years (Filene 2011a). For an exhibition at the North Carolina Collection Gallery at UNC-Chapel Hill (*Where Is Tobe? Unfolding Stories of Childhood, Race, and Rural Life*, 2014–2015), I set out to bring to the surface the multiple viewpoints embedded in a single

1930s photographic children's book about African American life—the story of the author, the photographer, the children who were the subjects of the photos, the publisher, the readers.

In each of these projects, key lessons were conveyed through incompleteness. In displaying our findings, we resolved to allow gaps to stand, to resist the temptation to fall back on generic fill-in information. In *Open House*, when we had only barebones information about the house's 1910s residents, we screen-printed just that fragmentary evidence onto uniforms representing each person's occupation. Hatmaker Doris Dahlstrom's features a large red ribbon with text from her entry in a 1918 *Industrial Survey of Women Employed Outside the Home*: "54 hours a week; wages—$9.00." When we found no details about the life of the original "Tobe" in several decades, the exhibition text noted that he "left only a few historical traces" in this period. Such silences reveal the unevenness and inequities in the historical record (Trouillot 1995, 26). They also invite visitors to consider how museum collections, too, are, necessarily, incomplete constructions. Silences leave room for visitors themselves to join in the interpretation, to ponder how to make sense of the gaps. The constructivist curator seeks multivalent objects, works to flesh out the multiple perspectives they suggest, and acknowledges that the task is never finished.

"Pre-constructed" Objects

If the constructivist collection prizes objects that open up the interpretive process, a special category of artifacts is those that are literally assemblages of interpretation—collections that people in the past put together to represent themselves. Think of time capsules or the objects sealed away in cornerstones. These truly are messages to the future from the past, even if the message is not always easy to decode. Typical time capsule holdings range from the technology of the moment (an electric toaster! microfilm!) to coins of the day, lists of the government officials who made a project possible, and, enticingly, letters expressing hopes and fears about what lies ahead.

These collections are not about the individual objects they contain but about the collective interpretation these things represent. This is our world, a time capsule says; do you recognize it? Time capsules, in other words, inherently represent the constructivist idea that assembling objects involves choices and point of view. These collections are "pre-constructed": their very form and content emerged from a series of highly visible interpretive decisions. Scrapbooks, as archivists have long understood, hold a similar appeal. Usually, the individual newspaper articles or photographs are unremarkable: the same or similar items can be found elsewhere. What gives a scrapbook power is that it offers us a glimpse into the mindset of the scrapbook-maker—the person wielding scissors and glue, deciding what to save to a page and what to toss aside.

The power and beauty of these "prefab" collections is that their interpretations are so clearly not static: their meaning demonstrably changes over time. Time capsules meant to represent the world to civilizations thousands of years hence look dated just decades later, as futuristic visions often turn out to be hopeless dead-ends. While the objects in the capsules haven't changed, their meaning has. Such interpretive dissonances and disconnects can show visitors how visions of history shift. The people assembling these collections made earnest efforts to make sense of their times, but we understand these periods differently now; no doubt, then, our own sense of past, present, and future is equally tenuous. Pre-constructed objects teach us—audiences and curators alike—how interpretation works and, along the way, give us all a useful dose of historical humility.

Not all pre-constructed collections are history-focused. In 1891, the Wagner Free Institute of Science in Philadelphia installed eighty-eight cherry-wood, glass-covered cases to hold 100,000 specimens representing the natural world, from rocks and minerals to taxidermied birds and mammals to the first saber-toothed cat skull found in North America. The cases have remained essentially unchanged ever since. As a result, the collection today can not only teach us about science but also about the world view of nineteenth-century scientists. The displays illustrate the naturalists' early understanding of evolution and, in some cases, their mistaken assumptions about species classifications. The collection becomes a way to show visitors how scientific knowledge itself evolves. For the museum today, the challenge is to interpret the gallery for visitors while preserving the integrity of the original collection: the display has become an artifact in itself.[1] Across town in Philadelphia, the Mütter Museum faced a similar challenge and opportunity with its collection of medical specimens. So did the Barnes Collection, whose idiosyncratic juxtapositions of art—arrangements mandated in the collector's will never to be altered—tell us as much about the aesthetic of Albert Barnes as about the original artists.

A collection frozen in time is unusual and, as the Barnes Collection's controversial move to central Philadelphia shows, even the eternal is not always forever. However, the dynamic of an institution's holdings being shaped by its founders is absolutely typical. Often, museums downplay the idiosyncrasy and power of their founders' vision, preferring to depict their work as dispassionately professional. Museums would be better served, though, by acknowledging that they were formed by people who had goals and values. As Fred Wilson showed in his startling *Mining the Museum* exhibition at the Maryland Historical Society (1992–1993), fresh questions can bring to the surface the interpretive assumptions in our collections.

Even without an outside provocateur, museums can reveal the constructed nature of their collections by emphasizing to visitors that our holdings have a history—not just an inanimate, institutional one that we mark with a centennial plaque, but a past driven by individuals with personalities and agendas. Sharing that story can clarify for visitors what we are up to in building our collections today. The constructivist collection not only shows objects in their places, but pulls back the curtain and invites visitors to consider who chose those objects and who set them in place (Weyeneth 2014, 23–24).

New Methods for Constructivist Collecting

Embracing the idea that collecting is a subjective act has implications not only for what one collects but also for the process of collecting. The question of who collects, for instance, becomes an interpretive decision in itself. In the constructivist museum, curators' personal perspectives and backgrounds are not pushed aside or glossed over but rather provide important access and understanding. The ongoing crisis of minority representation on museum staffs, then, becomes not only a problem of equity but also an inherent interpretive stumbling block. Recognizing that we are collecting in and for our time, we need to hear multiple voices and viewpoints. An inclusive conversation about perspectives and priorities is part of what we offer contemporary constituencies, and the terms of that conversation are what we pass on to the future through our collections.

The constructivist curator, then, sets out to facilitate conversations about interpretation and representation—a mission that reflects both a heightened awareness of our limits as collectors and an expanded sense of our possibilities. In collecting, we seek perspectives and recognize that the museum has no monopoly on them. In this light, community collaboration and visitor participation become not gimmicks but true opportunities. If we seek to understand the history of Latinx immigration to the American South, for instance, we might well ask recent immigrants what objects *they* see as representing that story. And we would collect not only the objects but also the immigrants' explanation of their significance. In 2008, to mark Minnesota's sesquicentennial, the Minnesota History Center asked residents to nominate people, places, and things that they felt represented 150 years of their state's history. Many of the selections (featured in the exhibition *MN150*) were ones that the curators would have chosen anyway, but the personal viewpoints provided—statements that were included in the exhibition along with the artifacts—brought new levels of meaning to the story. The Brooklyn Museum of Art famously applied crowd curation in its 2008 photography exhibition *Click!* First the museum issued an open call to artists to submit photos relating to the theme "Changing Faces of Brooklyn." Then, via an online forum, web visitors voted to select the top 20% for exhibition. Those images that received the most votes were printed the largest.

Such projects don't obviate the need for curatorial experts. For starters, it takes a great deal of expertise to pull off work like this. Staff members need to ask thought-provoking questions, facilitate inclusive discussion, and listen and adapt as the collaboration process unfolds (Filene 2011b, 12–13). A payoff is that participatory projects give visitors a sense of the myriad decisions involved in selecting and displaying artifacts: including-excluding, bigger-smaller, higher-lower, labeled-unlabeled, on and on. These decisions have *power*, and we want audiences to understand this fact. Our constituents don't resent experts, but they may well resent expertise exercised furtively, cloaked behind a veil of "best practices." The constructivist collection seeks transparency and legibility.

In considering how the mutability of knowledge affects museums, Simon J. Knell asserts that "If individuals construct their own sets of values, there is no such thing as a correct decision about what should be collected" (Knell 2004, 36). This sort of assessment might well be stymying, even a source of panic, to the thoughtful museum professional: In a world of radical relativism, how can we make any choices at all? Such despair, though, stems from a misunderstanding of constructivism's implications. Choices still matter, meaning is still made, some facts are still true and some "facts" plain false, some interpretations are richer and more nuanced than others. The constructivist collection does not mean anything goes. Instead, it demands being clearer about how objects carry meaning and how they don't. Museums need to embrace the idea that objects do not have inherent significance but, rather, convey the interpretations with which we imbue them. In the constructivist museum, we look for objects that can hold interpretive weight—those that allow for multiple meanings and juxtaposed perspectives, those that illustrate that interpretation is a time-bound, contested, and deeply human endeavor. We seek objects that do what we want our museums as a whole to do—offer rich, multilayered stories that enable challenging interpretations and empower visitors themselves to join in as interpreters. By setting aside our ambitions for the "eternal" collection, we can do work that makes museums more essential now and, as well, sends a more honest and powerful message about our world to the future.

Note

1 In 2013–2014, I worked with the Wagner staff on a project to prototype interpretive approaches in the gallery.

References

Barnett, Teresa. 2013. *Sacred Relics: Pieces of the Past in Nineteenth-Century America*. Chicago: University of Chicago Press.

Filene, Benjamin. 2011a. "Letting Go? Sharing Historical Authority in a User-Generated World." *History News* 66: 7–12.

Filene, Benjamin. 2011b. "Make Yourself at Home: Welcoming Voices in *Open House: If These Walls Could Talk*." In *Letting Go? Sharing Historical Authority in a User-Generated World*, edited by Bill Adair, Benjamin Filene, and Laura Koloski, 138–155. Philadelphia: Pew Center for Arts and Heritage/Left Coast Press.

Filene, Benjamin. 2017. "History Museums and Identity: Finding 'Them,' 'Me,' and 'Us' in the Gallery." In *Oxford Handbook on Public History*, edited by James Gardner and Paula Hamilton. New York: Oxford University Press.

Knell, Simon J. 2004. "Altered Values: Searching for a New Collecting." In *Museums and the Future of Collecting*, 2nd edition, edited by Simon J. Knell, 1–46. Burlington, VT: Ashgate Publishing.

McGlone, Patty. 2016. "African American Museum Visits American Heartland to Unearth Story of Free Black Farmers in the Early 19th Century." *Washington Post*, April 29. https://www.washingtonpost.com/news/arts-and-entertainment/wp/2016/04/29/

african-american-museum-visits-american-heartland-to-unearth-story-of-free-black-farmers-in-the-early-19th-century/.

Merriman, Nick. 2008. "Museum Collections and Sustainability." *Cultural Trends* 17(1): 3–19.

Post, Robert C. 2013. *Who Owns America's Past? The Smithsonian and the Problem of History*. Baltimore, MD: The Johns Hopkins University Press.

Rosenzweig, Roy and David Thelen. 1998. *The Presence of the Past: Popular Uses of History in American Life*. New York: Columbia University Press.

Schwarzer, Marjorie. 2012. *Riches, Rivals & Radicals: 100 Years of Museums in America*. Washington, DC: American Association of Museums.

Trouillot, Michel-Rolph. 1995. *Silencing the Past: Power and the Production of History*. Boston, MA: Beacon Press.

Weyeneth, Robert. 2014. "What I've Learned Along the Way: A Public Historian's Intellectual Odyssey." *The Public Historian* 36(2): 9–25.

A (PRACTICAL) INSPIRATION

Do You Know What It Costs You to Collect?

Trevor Jones

Collections Are Expensive, But We Don't Talk About It

If your museum has a permanent collection, every single item you acquire has an associated cost. It takes time and money to catalog, store, and preserve collections, and this cost is perpetual. Despite this fact, the actual cost of acquiring and storing collections is rarely considered by museum staff, directors, or boards. Many museum directors could tell you exactly what it costs to run an after-school program, but have no idea how acquiring a collection of farm tools will impact their bottom line. Collections staff are rarely asked to calculate what it costs to catalog and store museum collections, and this creates a dangerous blind spot for museum managers. American museums care for an estimated 500 million objects, but what does it cost to maintain all of these things (Heritage Preservation 2005)? The truth is, we don't know. The best (but incomplete) information comes from the United Kingdom where in 2008 Nick Merriman determined that a group of museums spent *an average of 60% of their resources on acquiring, storing and caring for collections* (Merriman 2008). That's a staggering figure, but can you prove it's lower for your institution?

Reluctance to discuss the costs of collecting may stem from a fear that any discussion of money and collections in the same breath will cause them to be seen as a financial asset. However, calculating the expense of cataloging and storing collections is not about the value of collections themselves, but rather the resources required to maintain them. I believe fiercely in the value of museum collections and their potential to create transformative experiences for visitors, but our collective failure to address the true costs of collecting has enabled museums to collect without fully understanding the repercussions of those decisions. At a time when resources for museums are stretched thin, it makes sense to know what it costs to catalog and store the collections that support our mission.

Calculating the Cost

I've dreamed of a "cost of collecting" calculator that would allow museum professionals to plug in a few key data points to calculate what it might cost to collect and store their artifacts.[1] Unfortunately this calculator doesn't yet exist, so when I was working at the Kentucky Historical Society I came up with a quick and dirty way to create a baseline for these costs.

My primary goal was to create a rough estimate, so I did not need to get too deep into the details. For example, I know that the likely cost to store and process an artifact or collection at the Kentucky Historical Society is as follows:

- It costs $16.50 per square foot per year to store an artifact.[2]
- It costs a minimum of $190 to accept an artifact, catalog it, and place it in storage.[3]

Thus, if a donor offers us a modest collection of 30 dolls that she played with as a child in Louisville, we can assume it will cost us about $5,700 in resources and staff and volunteer time to accession, catalog, and box the collection. If we estimate it will take five square feet to store, it will cost us $82.50 every single year to store this single collection. Storing it for 10 years (assuming a low 3% inflation rate and no other cost increases) will cost $945.74. Seeing those numbers quickly makes it apparent that if we take in this collection, we'd better be sure it supports the mission!

This is a rough estimate; it only takes into account some basic cost factors, and it's likely too low. It does not include the depreciation of our enameled storage cabinets, the cost of maintaining the freight elevator, or any number of other related expenses that go into maintaining a collections program.

A quick calculation of this type requires the following.

Determine the square feet of all the space you pay for (mortgage, rent, electric, utilities, maintenance), and then separate out the space you use for collections storage. If you've got good drawings you can work from those, but if not you can simply measure the space to calculate the total square footage. If you have a separate collections storage facility and your bills are separate for this building, it will simplify your task.

1. Calculate how many square feet of space you are using for collections storage. Use a map or a measurement for this, but don't get obsessed if it's an oddly shaped space, or you share part of it with other functions. Remember you're looking for a rough estimate. In my calculations I did not include any exhibition spaces, reasoning that collections in those spaces were playing a different role and were not really "stored."
2. Calculate your cost per square foot. If you rent space you'll likely have all the costs in a nice little bundle. If you don't have that, you'll need to look at your bills. If you already keep a monthly/quarterly or annual spreadsheet of physical

plant costs, you can total these up and divide the total by your total square footage. This will give you your cost per square foot.

3.   Multiply the cost per square feet by the number of square feet you use for collection storage. You will then know what it costs to store a square foot of material per year. This is probably as far as you need to go, but you can do more work to calculate the cost per cubic foot instead. It's likely you are not just storing collections in a single layer, but on high shelves. Start with the number of square feet of shelving and multiply that by the height of the shelving unit and you'll see how many cubic feet of potential storage space you have: (cubic feet) = (square feet) × (height in feet). Honestly, I looked at doing this for my storage areas, but it was just too complex. With storage spaces with shelving of different heights and different footprints, the calculations are more challenging and I just needed the baseline.

4.   Calculate your staff and equipment costs. Determine what it costs (per hour) for staff or volunteers to work with collections.[4] By tracking our team's progress with cataloging, I determined that it takes on average over five hours to accept, catalog, and store each newly accepted individual item or small archival collection. I also divided supply expenditures by the number of artifacts processed in a year. The result is an educated guess, as some resources get used for collections that are already in storage. You can get as detailed as you want with this process, but I chose not to go any deeper. I did not calculate the cost or depreciation for storage cabinets, insurance, database licenses, storage of digital images, or any number of other expenses. If you chose to do so, your costs will certainly be more accurate than mine.

Tell People What It Costs

Once your calculations are complete, it's vital that you share this information widely. Knowing that it costs $190 to catalog an item certainly helps focus discussions about what we bring into the collection! Even a rough estimate is a reminder that everything you acquire has a real and permanent cost. Paying $16.50 per square foot every year to store an artifact makes it clear that a collection must actively support the mission to be worth spending money on. It's also vitally important that management and board members understand the cost of collecting as well. Cost estimates help board members understand that collecting is an important (and expensive) part of what a museum does, and it also helps ensure that collections are not forgotten by management. After all, if we are paying to store these collections, we should develop programs that make good use of them.

Finally, it can also be beneficial to share costs with donors. The Kentucky Historical Society sends out every Deed of Gift with a letter stating:

> It takes at least five working hours to accept, catalog and store each accepted artifact. In today's costs, that's over $190 per item. *You have entrusted us with your treasure, now is your chance to help safeguard Kentucky's*

treasures forever. Please consider a gift to the Kentucky Treasures Fund so that all the Commonwealth's collections continue to receive the attention they deserve. In a time of declining state budgets, a gift to the Kentucky Treasures Endowment will make a lifetime of difference.

(Kentucky Historical Society n.d.; emphasis added)

Over the past several years, many signed Deed of Gift forms have been returned with checks. These are rarely major contributions, but the $100–250 donations add up. It turns out that if a donor has already entrusted you to care for an artifact that means something to them they are often eager to make a financial commitment to help support its long-term care.

Notes

1 The U.S. State Department has a list of over a dozen cost of living calculators at http://www.state.gov/m/fsi/tc/79700.htm. It would be great to have something similar to calculate the cost of storage!
2 Based on 2013–2014 actual operating expenses for the Kentucky Historical Society. Artifact storage encompasses 32,756 square feet. Total operating expenses for this space was $540,000. (This one is pretty easy as the state calculates rent on a square foot basis and heating and cooling costs are all included in this rate.)
3 It takes a minimum of five working hours to accept, catalog, and store each newly accepted item. The Kentucky Historical Society's average rate for personnel costs are $32/hour with the cost of benefits and retirement included. Supplies cost an average of $20 per new artifact based on our annual supply expenditures. This cost does not include expenses for storage cabinets, insurance, or costs to store master digital images of collections items. This cost is definitely a conservative estimate.
4 For volunteers you can use the Independent Sector rate $23.56 in 2015. https://www.independentsector.org/volunteer_time

References

Heritage Preservation and the Institute for Museum and Library Services. 2005. "A Public Trust at Risk: The Heritage Health Index Report on the State of America's Collections." Washington, DC: Heritage Preservation. http://www.heritagepreservation.org/HHI/summary.html.
Kentucky Historical Society. n.d. "Deed of Gift." Frankfort, KY.
Merriman, Nick. 2008. "Museum Collections and Sustainability." *Cultural Trends* 17(1): 3–21.

12

REWORKING COLLECTIONS MANAGEMENT PRACTICES FOR HOW WE MUST LIVE NOW

An Archival Case Study

Susan M. Irwin and Linda A. Whitaker

Introduction

Collect. Preserve. Interpret. Disseminate. How many times have you seen those words in a mission statement? For the history museum curator, archivist-librarian, or administrator, these tenets are the traditional ties that bind. While the mission of "collecting" stands at the core, it is the legacy practices surrounding collecting that haunt us (Ham 1984).

The authors of this chapter are certified archivists and librarians currently working in a history museum environment. Previously, we had specialized in processing and providing access to U.S. Congressional collections and related political materials. We have acquired a deep understanding of the emotionally, often politically charged environments generated both by the collections and by the archival practices surrounding them. We also know archival collections can run amok.

Which begs the question: How bad could archival collecting get? Answer: Bad enough to trigger a lawsuit when the stuff threatens the use and safety of a building where you are the tenant, not the owner.

We were hired in 2004 as the result of an out-of-court settlement caused by uncontrolled collecting. Our task was to fix archival management problems at the Arizona Historical Foundation (AHF), a private, non-profit repository founded by Senator Barry M. Goldwater and located within the Hayden Library at Arizona State University. We took a multi-focal, holistic approach discussed below under "The Cost of Collecting." This turned the tide for the archives but it was not enough to save the organization. The Foundation proved financially unsustainable for the long term and closed in June of 2012. As AHF was winding down, we were recruited by the Arizona Historical Society to find statewide management solutions for its archival collections. For six months, we had our feet in both worlds of endings and beginnings.

To fulfill our obligations at both locations meant challenging and overcoming the collections status quo, which we saw as legally, fiscally, and ethically untenable. The two situations demanded that we move in opposite directions. For the Arizona Historical Foundation, it meant closing down; for the Arizona Historical Society, it meant re-opening one of its branches and unifying archival practices statewide. In order to reach goals for both organizations, we had to take a tough look at the collections and reach out to our colleagues. This required considerable risk taking and the fundamental belief that change was not only possible, but also essential for how we as a field must live now.

When struggling with entrenched collections issues, working with colleagues is critical. We were lucky to find like-minded individuals who were willing to advocate for the greater good so that we could march forward together. We first joined the professional group, Arizona Archivists Roundtable, and later helped found the Arizona Archives Summit. In January 2009, the Summit's original participants—thirty professionals from universities, state archives, private organizations, tribal agencies, museums, and cultural centers—came together to re-write archives policies and procedures guided by three nationally recognized consultants. The immediate goals were to eliminate competition and duplication, increase access, and improve documentation of under-represented communities. The sense of a critical mass provided enough fuel to act on both the macro- and micro-levels.

We are not the first, nor will we be the last, to take a hard look at our disciplines and declare that we cannot go on doing this and expect that our collections management, public service, and relevancy will improve. We are sharing our archival experience in the hopes that those of you in the museum field might find our strategies applicable to your own collections work. What follows are summaries of the mindsets and actions taken to address legacy practices with an eye towards a more sustainable, accountable, and relevant future. We believe the wide-ranging actions described below address a number of "long list, big questions" put forward by the 2015 Future of Museums Collections Roundtable (Active Collections 2016).

A Failure of Stewardship

Some collections issues are so chronic, ingrained, and pernicious that they generate tolerance, apathy, and even paralysis, but the old saw "That's just how it is" will not cut it any longer (Sauer 2001, 332). Competition for collections, duplication, split collections, backlogs, lack of access, and lack of transparency are largely parasitic diseases that feed on their host institutions without killing them outright. More importantly, they leave a blueprint that is inherited by future generations. Is there a cure? Perhaps not, but for us the disease was rendered less toxic through a statewide collaborative model of collection management practices first proposed more than forty years ago (Fleckner 1976, 450). The mechanics for accomplishing this on a large scale have proven elusive largely because arriving at consensus can be the most difficult task in the world. Repositories must be willing to let go of the posturing and petty politics of the past in order to embrace a more sustainable collecting strategy that moves the field forward.

Arizona and Oregon were the first states to attempt a statewide collaborative approach to archival collecting. In Arizona, the movement towards archival collaboration was incremental, generated by the growing realization that our practices were hurting the very people we had pledged to serve (Whitaker and Sturgeon 2010, 11). Faced with the practical tasks of daily operations at the Arizona Historical Foundation and our own self-imposed benchmarks for processing collections, we looked certain legacy practices in the eye and said, "Enough." That line in the sand allowed us to navigate conflicting demands in a rapidly changing management environment. We found that relationship-building, timely reporting and shared inquiry provided a unique lens through which to analyze and meet a wide range of organizational needs. Bottom line: although we had a mandate to act, we could not implement big fixes in a vacuum. A community of practice was essential in building momentum for real change.

The initial mechanism for this change was the Arizona Archivist Roundtable. Under the auspices of the state archives, the roundtable began meeting annually in 2005. The idea was to bring together a broad spectrum of repositories to discuss issues of mutual interest and establish common ground. By 2007, a more complete picture of statewide collecting activities emerged as the result of one agenda item: How do we deal with hidden (i.e., unprocessed) collections?

Once we began discussing the issue of unprocessed collections with each other, the problems were jaw-dropping, the backlogs staggering, and the feedback from researchers deeply disturbing. Those most dependent on access to archival materials were also the most vulnerable: academics, students, writers for their livelihoods and credentials; immigrants for proof of citizenship; tribal members for water rights; and "down winders" in northern Arizona exposed to nuclear fallout in the 1950s. These researchers were generally reluctant to lodge complaints about access because they feared reprisals. They would accept limited access rather than risk denial of access altogether. Though anecdotal, here was evidence of archives as an essential, even lifesaving, service. Yet we failed to (1) advocate on our patrons' behalf; (2) advocate on our collections' behalf; (3) recognize that our own practices accounted for many of the problems; and (4) understand how we as stewards/gatekeepers of the historical record were perceived as potential threats to access. The reality of the archival landscape in Arizona was bleak. In 2008, the Great Recession had begun and every cultural institution in Arizona was under threat. At least ten repositories closed while others significantly reduced their hours. Despite the economic crisis, we resolved to turn this failure of stewardship around (Whitaker and Sturgeon, 14).

Guided by our own revised and approved policies and procedures, we re-evaluated, transferred, and de-accessioned collections at the Arizona Historical Foundation on a grand scale statewide. We also added core values to their strategic plan, i.e. *we will not collect what we cannot support*. We had the support of several governing bodies. We promised nothing that we could not deliver.

We were transparent. We were not sued. In short, we challenged a number of closely held beliefs that supported the tired policies and practices of the past and lived to tell about it.

Finding Common Ground—Fast

No one had the budget to plan or host a statewide meeting, but our consensus statements and goals caught the attention of the National Historical Publications and Records Commission (NHPRC). We consulted their grants staff and found we could meet the funding criteria. They were intrigued and watched this with interest. We were encouraged to apply and, nine years later, NHPRC continues to support our annual two-day meeting.

To succeed, this initiative demanded that Arizona's archival repositories transcend the culture of individualism and competition. Arizona's archivists are not numerous. We know each other well. The four original planners of the Archives Summit, however, had never put these issues on the table. Nor did we have the leisure for finely drawn philosophical debates. Reaching consensus on common issues required Arizona archivists to wrestle with controversies that have dominated the professional literature for years—issues that lie at the heart of ethical archival practice. These include, but are not limited to, collection acquisition and management, appraisal for research value, access to information, and backlogs.

How did the four original planners get to "yes?" Quicker than expected! In retrospect, more time was spent on defining unprocessed collections (no inventory, no finding aid) and what to post on the web (transparency, policies, lists of unprocessed collections) than on any other topic. There seemed to be a fundamental readiness for change and a general fatigue with institutional posturing. Our discussions were not divisive despite the sensitive topics, but consensus had to be reached if we were to get outside funding. Agreements to share data, to provide access to unprocessed collections, to post collection policies to websites, and to streamline processing techniques came fairly quickly. How was this possible?

First, access is an overriding core value for the archives profession. This is greatly influenced by the fact that the majority of practicing archivists today come out of library programs. Access to information is a library imperative. Framing the work of the Summit was the participants' commitment to access. Access promotes usefulness: it is what distinguishes an archive from a warehouse. For us, collecting has no purpose if no one has access to the material. While balancing access with preservation may be a struggle for some, the advent of digital technology allows archives to move the pendulum towards greater access (Society of American Archivists, 2016).

Second, the Summit planners understood and accepted that NHPRC funding was contingent on pledging to share information and adopt Greene and Meissner's "More Product Less Process" approach to processing backlogs (2005). Controversial at the outset, the idea of eliminating steps in processing won over many in the field. We were ready to adopt barebones description and minimal fussing with materials in favor of making the information available to researchers. More than anything else, this leveled the playing field for every participating repository across the state. Although controversial in some respects, we discovered that several repositories had been using a minimal processing approach for years without compromising long-term preservation.

Third, members of the Summit all had collection policies, but these were often dated, over-lapping, vague, and hidden. The price of admission to the Summit was that every participant had to submit their policies for review by a panel of consultants who also served as facilitators at the first meeting. Based on their feedback, several organizations made collection policy changes and others made their collections policy public on their repository's website (Arizona Historical Society 2012).

Fourth, we are driven by physical and intellectual control of our stuff. In archives, the common collection formats (e.g., manuscripts, ephemera, oral histories, photographs) are comparatively homogeneous and share similar storage requirements. Additionally, archival products come in standard sizes that fit most materials and shelving configurations. Assuming the HVAC is adequate, the collections can live next to each other in relative harmony. Further, archivists are masters of metadata and can provide access to collections (either processed or not) at the collection level. Aggregating information and avoiding item-level description is what we do. Moreover, this is what distinguishes archival practice from traditional librarianship.

Lastly, there is safety in numbers. If archival practice was to improve statewide, the major repositories had to move forward together. We were among the first to test this on a large scale. Tasked with resolving high profile, sometimes contentious, archival issues for two organizations, we leaned heavily on colleagues for advocacy, data, and collaborative problem solving.

The Big Reveal—Macro-Level

The revelations regarding unprocessed collections suggested a need for a more complete picture of archival holdings statewide. Could we create a database for unprocessed (hidden) collections? We could, although getting there required a lot of work, especially settling on controlled vocabulary (categories) for subject areas in an attempt to ensure quality and consistency of data entry. Summit participants contributed to a spreadsheet that captured collection basics: repository name, collection name, collection size, subject and geographic area, date range, whether it was processed/unprocessed, and whether or not it fit within an institution's collecting scope.

The result was the Summit Matrix, which provided a combined snapshot of repository holdings. A number of goals were served: (1) Archivists could assess their collections in context of the whole state. (2) Under and over-documented areas (too much Old West, not enough New West), repository strengths, and split collections became readily apparent. No longer collecting in isolation, participating organizations could now modify their collecting scopes to promote inclusion, diversity, and community identity. (3) An objective platform was provided for making donor referrals. What was once a random occurrence became a routine collaboration between archival repositories. (4) Almost overnight, 98% of unprocessed collections, or 21,007 linear feet, were made available to the research public (Arizona Summit Archives n.d.).

The Cost of Collecting—Micro-Level

Our experiences with the Arizona Summit soon proved invaluable in successfully navigating an example of unbridled collecting. As stated previously, the authors were hired by the Arizona Historical Foundation (AHF) in 2004 as the result of a legal settlement triggered by its collecting practices. Unencumbered by a collecting policy, materials accrued at an unbridled rate. As the collections metastasized and encroached on library space, tensions mounted. Donors and researchers became increasingly dissatisfied with unfulfilled promises and inaccessible research materials. The result was a legally binding agreement to hire professional staff (us) in order to gain physical and intellectual control of the collections.

First, we declared a moratorium on collecting and made all collections—processed and unprocessed—accessible. We then developed a sustainable collection policy. We followed these steps by returning or reuniting a number of contested collections that AHF did not own. Although we were able to demonstrate quick and quantifiable outcomes, these did not guarantee longevity.

What we did not see coming was a financial crisis compounded by debt, the downturn in the economy, and the repository's inability to raise sufficient revenue. It soon became clear that the Foundation needed to shut down operations. Hired as archivists, we did not have shutting down the entire operation as part of our original plan. We chose to stay because we were committed to responsible stewardship. For us, this was an ethical imperative: identifying the best possible homes for these collections lay at the heart of those responsibilities.

We switched gears and with considerable board advocacy and support secured a grant from a private foundation. This bought us time and goodwill. The AHF board accepted and understood that this reprieve was temporary. We secured three years of funding to get the AHF's affairs in order and find homes for over 6,000 linear feet of library and archival collections. Overnight, our roles were fundamentally transformed. (1) Functionally, we were given parity with the thirty-member board who deferred all decisions to us from that point forward. (2) We went from the roles of staff archivists to that of major donors of collections to Arizona's repositories. The Arizona Summit experience provided the network, the context, and the objective criteria from which to make decisions. We were able to identify where each collection would have the most relevance and usefulness. This was a collaborative, problem-solving process within what has become a tight-knit archival community.[1]

Epilogue

We are happy to report that our archivist team landed on its feet. In 2012, we were hired by the Arizona Historical Society at Papago Park to re-open a branch that had been closed for over four years and to standardize and improve archival collection management at all Society locations: Flagstaff, Tucson, Yuma, and Tempe. This remains a work in progress. It is a tale of winnowing and gathering from within, rather than statewide dispersal. That story can be told another time but the principles remain the same. We have a bias towards action. We declare moratoriums on collecting when backlogs exceed 20% of total linear feet of holdings. We make everything accessible, whether it is processed or not. We have removed entire collections, processed them far from their homes, and returned them to the community that created them. We have been transparent throughout. The big takeaways are these: Do not be afraid to challenge the status quo, but take the time to consult your colleagues. At the Arizona Archives Summit we discovered repeatedly that there was common ground among archivists wrestling with the same issues we were. Our meetings over the years established a community of practice in which we adopted strategies that helped repositories of all sizes. By being both bold and collaborative, we were able to promote change not only in how things were done in our workplaces, but across the state.

The archival profession was warned over sixty years ago that we were in an era of increasing volume and decreasing uniqueness. We largely ignored these warnings to carefully select and continually evaluate what we collected and preserved (Schellenberg 1959, 54). Most collecting policies are so broadly written that they invite duplication, competition, and indiscriminate acquisition. This begs the question: How do you distinguish your stuff from the other collecting institutions in the same city, county, or state?

While we cannot predict what the future will deem important, we are aware of the shortcomings of the past. The need for inclusivity, community connections, and compelling storytelling has never been greater. This in fact helps define uniqueness. In an environment of declining funding, limited storage space, understaffed organizations, and increasing amounts of material to collect, it is imperative that we collect smartly and manage resources with surgical precision. What we can do is choose materials that are relevant and representative of communities today so that they provide insights for future generations. We can minimize duplication, decrease competition, increase collaboration, diversify collections, and share information. We can refine and re-focus our collection policies. By doing these things, we can demonstrate that collecting institutions are an essential public service.

Note

1 To see where the collections landed, visit http://www.ahfweb.org/.

References

Active Collections. 2016. "Future of Museum Collections Roundtable." http://www. activecollections.org/roundtable/.

Arizona Historical Society. 2012. Collections Policy. http://www.arizonahistoricalsociety. org/wp-content/upLoads/CollectionsPolicy_Approved2012.pdf.

Arizona Summit Archives n.d. Unprocessed Collections. https://azarchivesmatrix.org/ matrix-results/unprocessed/.

Fleckner, John A. 1976. "Cooperation as a Strategy for Archival Institutions." *American Archivist* 39(4): 447–459.

Greene, Mark A. and Dennis Meissner. 2005. "More Product, Less Process: Revamping Traditional Archival Processing." *American Archivist* 68(2): 208–263.

Sauer, Cynthia K. 2001. "Doing the Best We Can? The Use of Collection Development Policies and Cooperative Collecting Activities at Manuscript Repositories." *American Archivist* 64(2): 308–349.

Schellenberg, Theodore. 1959. "The Future of the Archival Profession." *American Archivist* 22(1): 49–58.

Society of American Archivists. 2016. "Core Values and Code of Ethics Statement." http:// www2.archivists.org/statements/saa-core-values-statement-and-code-of-ethics.

Whitaker, Linda A. and Melanie I. Sturgeon. 2010. "The Arizona Summit: Tough Times in a Tough Land." *Journal of Western Archives* 1(1): 2–28. http://digitalcommons.usu.edu/ westernarchives/vol1/iss1/3.

Selected Readings

Arizona Historical Foundation. 2012a. Collections Processed. http://www.ahfweb.org/ collections_processed.html.

Arizona Historical Foundation 2012b. Photograph Collections. http://www.ahfweb.org/ collections_photographs.htm.

Coyner, Libby and Pringle, Jonathan. 2014. "Metrics and Matrices: Surveying the Past to Create a Better Future." *American Archivist* 77(2): 459–488.

Ericson, Timothy L. 1991. "At the Rim of Creative Dissatisfaction: Archivists and Acquisition Development." *Archivaria* 33: 66–77.

Greene, Mark A. 2002. "What Were We Thinking? A Call to Embrace Reappraisal and Deaccessioning." *Provenance* 20(1): 33–49.

———. 2006. "I've Deaccessioned and Lived to Tell About It: Confessions of an Unrepentant Reappraiser." *Archival Issues* 30: 7–22.

Ham, F. Gerald. 1984. "Archival Choices: Managing the Historical Record in an Age of Abundance." *American Archivist* 47(1): 11–22.

Rapport, Leonard. 1981. "No Grandfather Clause: Reappraising Accessioned Records." *American Archivist* 44(2): 143–150.

Zinn, Howard, 1977. "Secrecy, Archives, and the Public Interest." *The Midwestern Archivist* 2(2): 14–26.

13

OBJECT REINCARNATION

Imagining a Future Outside the Permanent Collection

Kate Bowell

Introduction

Tamiko stood towards the back of the room, watching the students bent over tables as they worked on their items. The museum had hosted plenty of "Take Apart Days" before, but always with items donated by the public and scrounged up by volunteers. Visitors loved disassembling old VCRs and dissecting Rubik's Cubes to see how they worked. But today was different. Today, the participants were not taking apart things from a neighbor's basement, but objects from the museum's collection.

The idea first began to form as Tamiko and two of her coworkers were spending months reorganizing the museum's back collection, a storage space where staff seldom entered and objects rarely left. Realizing how many objects had been accessioned and then never touched again, they started imagining other ways the objects could be used. It was Tamiko who came up with the idea of letting visitors get their hands on them—literally.

It was difficult to get the collections managers and curators to even consider the idea but, eventually, the museum selected twelve pieces to deaccession and deconstruct. The students dismantling the objects were sophomores from a local high school. Two years before, the museum began a curriculum partnership with the school district. Lectures, labs, courses, and internships allowed students to use the museum and its collections to extend their learning beyond the classroom.

The students were focused as they explored their objects, checked the reference books the curator and collections manager had provided, talked with their partners about what they saw, and called museum staff over when they had questions. By taking the objects apart, the students were learning how they had been put together and exploring the fundamental questions of who had made them, needed them, used them, and, most importantly, why that information mattered. Exploring these objects intimately helped bring the past closer and make it as tangible as the pieces the students held in their hands.

For the moment this was a one-off event, an experiment. But it was a start, Tamiko thought to herself. Museums should be a place for experiments.

At any given moment, the majority of a typical museum's collection is in storage rather than on display. The percentage of exhibited objects varies, but is generally between 1% and 5% of a total collection (Fabrikant 2009). The other 95–99% largely consists of objects that are earmarked for possible future exhibition, in education collections, on loan to other organizations, too fragile for display, or primarily used for research. However, even after accounting for all those uses, most museums still have leftover items.

Often, these neglected artifacts are the unloved objects that exist on the fringes of collections. They do not actively support missions, but are passively and permanently kept because of protocol, not purpose. Most current collection guidelines leave museums with few options for the future of these challenging objects. Much of the time, collection restrictions result in these items staying where they are and providing little or no active value to museums and their communities—not because the objects are inherently valueless, but because their value cannot be easily realized within the museums stewarding them.

Museums could free these objects from permanent collection purgatory. Instead of being relegated to the backs of cabinets and the bottoms of shelves, unloved collection pieces could be released, revitalized, and reincarnated outside museums. They could go to new places, be used in new ways, and have new meanings for the people who experience them.

Imagining these possibilities invites unconventional ideas about stewardship and the permanence of collections. These ideas encourage and challenge museums to critically examine objects through new perspectives, to ask questions, and, ultimately, to counter the stagnation of modern collections by encouraging the flow of objects out of them. What that outflow could look like, and what it could mean for the ways museums and communities understand, support, and interact with one another via objects, is the main focus of this thought-experiment.

Original Contexts—A Return to the Beginning

Make New Connections by Returning Objects to Old Locations

Instead of displaying items away from their original contexts, museums could put objects back where they came from.

Most museums are fundamentally artificial constructions: objects inside them are held outside time and space, suspended within a specific perspective. It is not an inherently incorrect approach, but it results in visitor-object engagement that is mediated through layers of created, rather than organic, narratives. However, when museums offer visitors the opportunity to encounter objects in situ (or, at least, "near situ"), the mediation changes and opportunities for visitor understanding and connection are enhanced.

This is already done in museums associated with significant sites. From seeing George Washington's dentures displayed at Mount Vernon to marveling at the preserved remains of a prehistoric camel at the La Brea Tar Pits, museums built around significant locations give visitors the opportunity to experience objects in relation to their original settings. Location becomes an integral piece of the narrative and objects are enhanced by the additional meaning imparted by a connection to place. However, historic homes, prehistoric tar pits, and other location-specific museums often work on a large scale, exhibiting big stories with multiple objects. Imagine what could happen on a small scale if museums returned individual objects to their original locations, sprinkling them throughout a community.

Not every bank had a fossil ammonite mounted next to the ATM, Suzanne thought. And not just the bank, either. The pharmacy had a big nautilus shell in its window and there was a display of trilobites in the lobby of the gym down the street. Their town had turned into its own science exhibit.

After the state natural history museum had inventoried its collections a few years earlier, a curator approached their community with a proposal. The museum had a small assortment of fossils collected from the area in the 1920s. The pieces were nice, but the museum had more detailed and intact specimens from the same locations. These fossils hadn't been exhibited or studied in decades. Would the town be interested in having them back? Suzanne was surprised when she learned that the fossils belonged to aquatic animals. Living in a dry climate, she assumed the fossils would be parts of dinosaurs. But millions of years ago, their corner of the state was the edge of an inland sea and it was remains of that marine life that the museum shared.

Originally, the plan was to exhibit the fossils in the local museum, but students at the high school had another idea. They went to the state museum, looked through the specimens' records, and mapped out where each fossil was found. Then the students went to the local organizations closest to those locations and convinced most of them to display the associated pieces. By the end of that school year more than thirty organisms were, in a way, back where they came from. This year, several high school seniors were working on a project to write labels for the fossils and produce a self-guided tour. Now, walking down Main Street was like walking back in time and people were enjoying their town's history—all 100 million years of it.

Community Ownership—An Exercise in Trust

Invert the Relationship of Museums, Trust, and Community

Instead of museums holding objects in trust for communities, museums could trust communities to hold objects for themselves.

Many of the most common museum practices, from employing security guards to banning flash photography, exist to protect objects from visitors. Even the act of accessioning an item into a museum, instead of leaving it with the public, speaks to an assumption that the average person isn't capable of caring for precious objects. Museums mediate visitor-object interactions with labels and lectures and vitrines and velvet ropes because, on some significant level, museums don't trust their visitors.

Of course, this attitude isn't unfounded. On occasion, visitors allowed to get too close have almost urinated on paintings (Clyfford Still's *1957-J2*) (Miller 2012), irreversibly "restored" frescos (Elías García Martínez's *Ecce Homo*) (Minder 2012), and shattered parts of glass sculptures (Shelly Xue's *Angel is Waiting*, since renamed *Broken*) (Loughrey 2016). Museums are, understandably, on the defensive, but this attitude has created additional problems. In the modern museum hierarchy of value, protection often trumps connection and visitors are kept at a distance from the very objects with which museums are encouraging them to engage. Museums can change this dynamic, however, and create new hierarchies of value by offering visitors valuable things.

British artist Clare Twomey explored this idea in *Trophy*, her 2007 installation at the Victoria & Albert Museum. By creating and then scattering 4,000 Wedgwood jasperware birds through the Cast Courts, Twomey curated a space where people could form immediate and intimate connections with pieces of art. Visitors touched the birds, picked them up, and, without prompting from Twomey or the museum, took them. Five hours after the exhibit opened all the birds were gone (Twomey 2016; Crows Nest Films 2013). *Trophy* created objects to be taken, but museums already have objects to give away. People are capable of caring for precious things and making the things they care for precious. Imagine what could happen if museums let them.

Martina's year was almost done. She held up the old coffee pot, taking one long last look before setting it down, uploading one more photo to Instagram, and tagging it with #objectsoutsidethemuseum. "Last day," she wrote. "It's a little weird that I don't want to say goodbye, right?"

For the past 12 months, the coffee pot had been hers. She had not been a regular coffee drinker before, but having the pot changed that. She liked the ritual of using it each weekend and this piece of history had become part of her routine. But soon it would go to someone else, ready to fill their kitchen with that lovely, rich, slightly bitter smell.

Martina smiled as she remembered her surprise when she first heard about the local history museum's "Call for Receivers." The museum was giving artifacts away? Well, sort of. These were objects in need of a good home and any object you "adopted" was yours for a year. You were free to actually use the object you were given—in fact, it was encouraged—but you also signed an agreement promising to be responsible for the object's care and to share it with your community. It was the sharing that had excited Martina. Whether it was through social media or knocking on your neighbor's door, you were required to reconnect the object with a piece of the world as big or small as you chose.

Martina checked the time—people would begin arriving soon. Each year before the items were returned and redistributed, the museum produced a tour map of the object receivers throughout the town. More than just a list of places and items, the map included stories about the objects and their custodians. Martina was curious and a little nervous about what it would be like to open her home as a mini "museum for a day," but mostly she was excited. Today, she would make coffee and invite visitors to sit and chat as they enjoyed each other's company and the object that brought them together. Tomorrow, she would return the pot to the museum, add her tweets, posts, and journaling entries to the object's growing biography, and receive something new to care for. She was curious about what she would adopt next, but for now she looked forward to one more day feeling the coffee pot's weight and warmth in her hands.

Artistic Rebirth—A Reinvention of Identity

Give Objects New Lives by Giving Them Over to People with New Visions

Instead of establishing the meanings of objects through cataloguing and labeling, museums could invite artists to reimagine and reinvent objects as something else.

A primary function of museums is to answer the question, "What is it?" By defining objects within set knowledge boundaries, museums assert expertise over object identity and lock objects into a single story. However, if people outside museums were invited to enhance, contribute to, or even redefine these identities, items could be given lives outside the expected museum narrative and objects could be experienced, appreciated, and known in a new light.

In 2008, in partnership with the Zuiderzeemuseum and W139 art gallery, Dutch artist Zoro Feigl combed the museum's permanent collection for unused objects that could be transformed. The resulting installation, *Breakers*, presented a maritime scene of a lighthouse surrounded by rough waves, all created out of "household items, art objects, and machines from the collection" (Zuiderzeemuseum 2008; Feigl 2016). In Feigl's piece, upended boats became a lighthouse, waving ropes became the sea, and magnet-influenced compasses became unreliable navigators. By manipulating and reimagining the items he used, Feigl redefined the objects and freed them to tell a new story.

In *Breakers* and similar "reimagined meaning" installations, the changes to object identity are temporary. Ultimately, each item goes back into the collection and reverts to what it was before. Imagine what could happen if museums offered opportunities for lasting identity change and encouraged artists and creators to transform objects into something new, permanently.

Victor looked around the open workspace. As an artist, the hum of potential and possibility that was tangible throughout the room invigorated him. As a curator, that same energy made him nervous.

It had started out small. Years ago, the art and history museum Victor worked for commissioned a temporary installation displaying objects from the museum's permanent collection in new and creative ways. The exhibit was a success and for the past six years the museum had featured similar exhibits using objects that visitors might never otherwise see.

Last year, an artists' collective proposed taking the idea further: rather than a temporary exhibit, why not a permanent transformation of some museum objects into new things for the community? They were reluctant at first, with months of discussion over whether or not the museum could even consider *deaccessioning any objects and then, after they agreed, there had been a thorough vetting process to determine which pieces could be let go. Next were meetings with the artists, introducing them to the objects and their stories. But now here they all were—museum staff, artists, and objects alike—and something new was happening.*

Over in one corner stood a pile of old handkerchiefs, pillowcases, and other linens—a few of which were more holes than cloth—ready to be cut apart. The small pieces of fabric were being appliqued with other materials to form a quilt. Four women sat around the base, talking and laughing as they built repeating patterns out of the scraps. When it was finished, the quilt would go to a local women's support shelter. Victor had spoken with the artists and was impressed at their intent to connect the tradition of quilting bees, acts of communal creation where women helped and supported one another, with this act of creation and the support it would give other women.

Across the room he saw Katharine, the museum's director, deep in conversation with a mosaic artist. Surrounded by small medicine vials—thousands of them came into the museum's collection after an old pharmacy had closed—the artist was showing Katharine a technique to cut the glass into rings and tiles. He was working on two pieces, one of which was promised for the lobby of the local middle school, while the other would be auctioned off to raise funds for the collective and the museum.

Victor would be lying if he said that he was completely comfortable watching museum objects being dismantled and deconstructed. This was not how he had been trained to see, or steward, collections. But he also saw that something special—and important—was beginning. These artists were doing for the pieces what the museum had not: breathing new life into old objects and sending them back out into the world.

Cathartic Destruction—An Acceptance of Impermanence

Acknowledge the Idea That Certain Objects Should Not Last Forever

Instead of preserving objects in perpetuity, museums could embrace the idea that some objects should decay, deteriorate, or even be destroyed.

This is a highly controversial idea; museums are meant to hold objects indefinitely. But most objects are not meant to last that long. The concept of preservation suspends items in stasis instead of letting them complete a lifecycle of use, repair, and replacement. Within this mindset, an object's value is dependent upon its permanence. However, if museums acknowledged the value in an object's impermanence, they could redefine the understanding of object worth altogether.

In 1995, Chinese artist Ai Weiwei released *Dropping a Han Dynasty Urn*, a photographic triptych of himself holding, releasing, and shattering an ancient ceramic vase ("Artistic License" 2012). Seventeen years later, in 2012, Swiss artist Manuel Salvisberg echoed Ai's piece with *Fragments of History*. In that work, art collector Uli Sigg is shown holding, releasing, and shattering *Coca-Cola Urn*, another Han Dynasty urn that Ai had previously painted with the Coca-Cola logo (Jones 2014). Destroying the original urns did not negate their value, but rather enabled that value to be incorporated into something else. In both instances, the destruction of old objects allowed for the creation of new art.

If there is value in destruction when the act generates something new, there may also be value when the act creates an experience, rather than a tangible product. At times, the provocative, emotional, cleansing, or cathartic nature of an object's active destruction may be more valuable than its preservation. Imagine what could happen if museums committed not only to identifying opportunities to transfer object ownership to individuals or communities, but also committed to supporting the recipients in deciding whether or not those objects should be preserved or destroyed.

Jonathan looked down at the sheaf of papers in his hand. The 50-year-old ink was faded and the yellowed paper had tears and holes along the folds that grew each time the delicate sheets were handled. The papers had been destined for the trash pile, but now they were heading to the burn pile.

He still couldn't quite believe that the civic museum had approached the community group he led and offered to give them these pamphlets and leaflets with no strings attached. At first, Jonathan and some of the other members had thought about keeping the materials and preserving them as part of the history they shared. But the museum had the same materials in better condition in its archives, and everything was also digitized and accessible online. So he called a community meeting, put the fate of the papers to a vote, and a consensus was reached. The papers would be burned in an act of defiance and control.

Now, as a crowd stood around the bonfire, Jonathan passed out the papers. By firelight, the pale print from the 1960s was still legible and the sentences decrying the dangers of school integration within their city almost seemed to jump off the page. After a moment, each person dropped their piece into the fire, watching as the dry sheets disintegrated into nothing but smoke, dissipating into the sky.

Jonathan knew this gesture didn't erase history, literally or figuratively. Burning pamphlets didn't forgive or ignore the racism or injustice that so many people had suffered, nor did it end the battles they were still fighting today. All those moments happened, and were happening. But what they came together to do around the bonfire was happening, too, and the symbolism of destroying the efforts of people who had worked so hard to discount and demean them wasn't lost on anyone. They would carry the memory of this moment with them as they kept moving forward. It didn't change the past and it wasn't going to singlehandedly change the future, but that didn't mean it wasn't part of a change.

Conclusion

The alternative futures for unloved objects imagined here are strongly informed by the present situations of many museums. Currently, caring for objects that do not support their missions has created a burden of obligation for museums that does a disservice to the organizations, their visitors, and objects alike. Museums are in the position to determine the futures of the objects in their custody, and that means that they have the opportunity to choose something different.

What is encouraging and exciting is that the scenarios envisioned here are extensions of strategies already happening in some museums. Many museums and their audiences are exploring new ways to engage with one another and create moments of meaning that transcend the traditional museum-object-visitor model. However, the object futures proposed here may not work in all contexts or communities. There is no guarantee that innovative ideas will always be successful, but the current scale and scope of maintaining unused objects in museum collections is unsustainable. The goal of these alternatives is not to produce a prescriptive outline for museums to follow when faced with the dilemma of unloved objects, but to encourage museums to ask fundamental questions about those objects: Why are they here? What can they do in this museum? What will their futures be if they stay? What could their futures be if they go?

The first step toward answering these questions is to approach collections with a new perspective. Rather than considering unloved and un(der)used objects with a sense of obligation, try examining them through a lens of opportunity. Where could these objects be useful, valued, helpful, or loved? By breathing new life into old objects, what groups could museums reach and what connections could they foster? How could a shift from defining objects as things to be *viewed* by the public to one of defining objects as things to be *used* by the public benefit museums, individuals, and communities alike?

Objects that do not, or cannot, serve a purpose in the collections they inhabit should have the opportunity to be reincarnated into something meaningful somewhere else, and museums can help facilitate that transformation. Reincarnation is, by its very nature, dramatic, monumental, emotional, and daunting. It is no easy thing for museums to relinquish control, set objects free, and help them assume a new identity. Over time, however, this may become easier as more museums begin to explore and experiment with what this process could look like and mean. If museums can acknowledge the notion of object impermanence and accept the idea that the collection is not always an object's final home, we may see those pieces have extraordinary new lives. In the end, it may not be just objects that are reincarnated, but perhaps even the concept of the museum itself.

References

"Artistic License." 2012. *The Economist*, May 5. http://www.economist.com/node/21554178.

Crows Nest Films. 2013. "Trophy at the V&A." Vimeo, March 28. https://vimeo.com/62861350.

Fabrikant, Geraldine. 2009. "The Good Stuff in the Back Room." *New York Times*, March 12. http://www.nytimes.com/2009/03/19/arts/artsspecial/19TROVE.html.

Feigl, Zoro. 2008. "De Branding/The Breakers." http://www.zorofeigl.nl/de-branding-the-breakers/.

Jones, Jonathan. 2014. "Who's the Vandal: Ai Weiwei or the Man Who Smashed His Han Urn?" *The Guardian*, February 16. https://www.theguardian.com/artanddesign/jonathanjonesblog/2014/feb/18/ai-weiwei-han-urn-smash-miami-art.

Loughrey, Clarisse. 2016. "Children Destroy Glass Art Installation as Adults Film Them." *The Independent*, May 24. http://www.independent.co.uk/arts-entertainment/art/news/children-destroy-glass-art-installation-as-adults-film-them-a7044596.html.

Miller, Leigh Anne. 2012. "Woman Arrested for Drunkenly Punching Clyfford Still Painting." *Art in America*, January 4. http://www.artinamericamagazine.com/news-features/news/clyfford-still-attacked/.

Minder, Raphael. 2012. "Despite Good Intentions, a Fresco in Spain Is Ruined." *New York Times*, August 23. http://www.nytimes.com/2012/08/24/world/europe/botched-restoration-of-ecce-homo-fresco-shocks-spain.html.

Twomey, Clare. 2006. "Trophy." http://www.claretwomey.com/trophy.html.

Zuiderzee Museum. 2008. "Breakers in Museum." March 17. http://www.zuiderzeemuseum.nl/en/132/news/breakers-in-museum/?id=89.

EPILOGUE

Imagine with Us

Rainey Tisdale

The Active Collections team has started playing around with "alternative universe" scenarios, hoping they might help us imagine new possibilities for museum collections in the real world. How might the following alterations to the assumptions that govern collections hold positive potential, not only for everyday museum practice but also for the public value museums provide to society? And what additional scenarios can *you* imagine?

- What if museums were barred by law from *owning* the objects they work with?
- What if museums functioned like a branch of medicine, and objects were prescribed to cure what ails you?
- What if museums functioned like lending libraries, and objects circulated through communities like books?
- What if museums functioned like reference libraries or hardware stores that help you answer questions or solve problems?
- What if there were a museum acquisitions version of affirmative action, where collections were required to proportionately reflect the communities they serve?
- What if every object came with user ratings (1–5 stars), thumbs up/thumbs down buttons, reviews/comments, and a record of every transformative experience it had produced?
- What if deaccessioned objects got a goodbye ceremony that helped us bless and release them with a greater sense of ritual and closure?
- What if curators weren't assigned to specific collections but instead served at-large, choosing objects and ideas to work with from many different collections?
- What if we built a museum—and its collection—totally from scratch, based on the needs of a twenty-first-century audience, without any of the history, baggage, or practical constraints of the museums we have today? What would it look like?

INDEX